# birds

## 20 jewelry and accessory designs

*by Sophie Robertson*

DEUTSCHE BUNDES PO 10₄
50 JAHRE DEUTSCHES MUSEUM

THE GUILD OF MASTER CRAFTSMAN PUBLICATIONS

First published 2013 by
Guild of Master Craftsman Publications Ltd
Castle Place, 166 High Street, Lewes,
East Sussex BN7 1XU

Text and illustrations © Sophie Robertson, 2013
Copyright in the Work © GMC Publications Ltd, 2013

ISBN 978 1 86108 976 2

A catalogue record for this book is available
from the British Library.

Set in King and Myriad
Color origination by GMC Reprographics
Printed and bound in China

Publisher Jonathan Bailey
Production Manager Jim Bulley
Managing Editor Gerrie Purcell
Senior Project Editors
Cath Senker and Sara Harper
Managing Art Editor Gilda Pacitti
Photographer Andrew Perris
Designer Rob Janes

birds

# contents

Continued...

FEATHERY

SONGBIRD

SILHOUETTE

FLIGHT

BEADY

WISDOM

DECOUPAGE

CHARM

# The Projects

STAMP

PEARLY

PEACOCK

NIGHT OWL

VICTORIANA

ELEGANCE

FLAMINGO

STREAMLINED

CHIRPY

SPARKLY

VINTAGE

RETRO

# Tools

THE FOLLOWING PAGES WILL GIVE YOU A GOOD IDEA OF SOME OF THE MOST USEFUL TOOLS AVAILABLE TO HELP YOU MAKE THE PROJECTS IN THIS BOOK, AND ALSO THE KIND OF MATERIALS YOU WILL NEED.

## pliers and cutters

Pliers are needed for most projects; the ones listed here are essential for the projects in this book. Cutters are essential for working with chain, wire, or fabric. Remember to use the correct type for the material you are cutting.

### FLAT-NOSE PLIERS

These have flat parallel jaws that don't taper. They are useful for bending and flattening wire, squeezing ribbon crimps, and also holding, opening, and closing jumprings and other findings.

### ROUND-NOSE PLIERS

These have completely round jaws that taper to a point at the end. They are used for making eyepins and bending wire into loops, coils, and spirals.

### SNIPE-NOSE PLIERS

Also called chain-nose pliers, these pliers have half-round jaws on the outside with flat parallel faces on the inside. They taper from a wider base to smaller tip. Their small tip makes them very useful for holding, opening, and closing small components and jumprings.

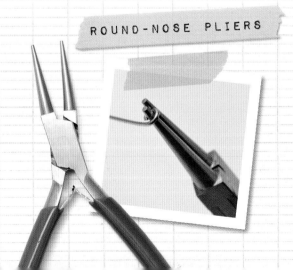

ROUND-NOSE PLIERS

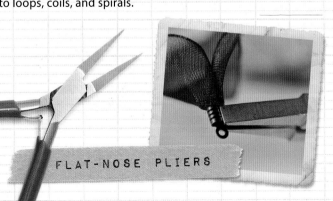

FLAT-NOSE PLIERS

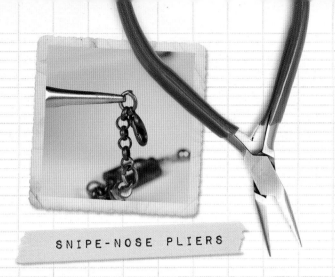

SNIPE-NOSE PLIERS

## FABRIC SCISSORS

Specialized scissors with extremely sharp blades, these are designed for cutting fabric. Do not cut anything other than fabric with them, as this will blunt the blades.

## GENERAL-PURPOSE SCISSORS

Scissors that have a fine, long nose so that you can reach into small areas, and are sharp so that you can accurately cut fabric and paper.

## EMBROIDERY SCISSORS

Small scissors with sharp tips that can trim threads neatly and accurately.

## END CUTTER

The cutter is at the end of this tool and is suitable for cutting thin materials, wire, and chain. The design of this tool lets you get right up close to your design to snip off any excess wire and leave you with a flush finish.

## SIDE CUTTER

This is similar to an end cutter but the cutter runs along the side. The tip is handy for getting into small spaces such as the individual links of small chain.

GENERAL-PURPOSE SCISSORS

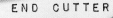

EMBROIDERY SCISSORS

FABRIC SCISSORS

END CUTTER

SIDE CUTTER

# needles

These are available in many different types and sizes for hand sewing, and the material and thread you are using will determine the type you need. Needle sizes are specified by numbers, with the higher the number meaning the finer the needle. For the most basic hand sewing you will only really need two types.

## SHARPS

These are the most commonly used needles on all sorts of hand-sewing projects. They are medium length, have sharp points, and come in sizes 1–12.

## GLOVERS

These have a triangular point so they can pierce and sew through tough materials like leather, suede, denim, and plastics. They come in sizes 1–10.

## NEEDLE THREADER

This helpful little tool is a silver tab with a wire diamond-shape loop. You put the loop of the needle threader through the eye of the needle, thread the cotton through the loop, and pull the loop back out of the eye of the needle, bringing the cotton with it.

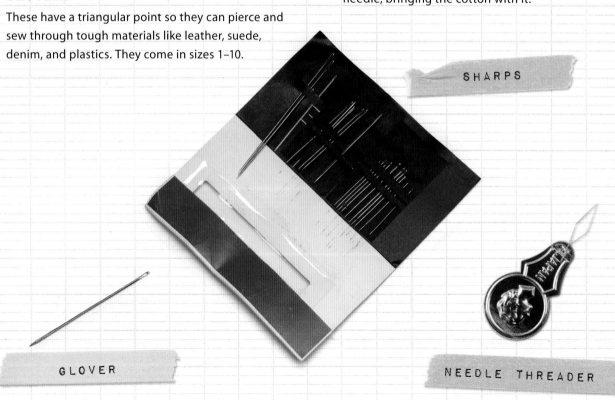

SHARPS

GLOVER

NEEDLE THREADER

# miscellaneous tools

Below is a collection of tools that feature in the following projects but are also very handy to keep around for future tasks. They are available from craft or hardware stores, and online retailers.

## MIXING STICKS

Long wooden sticks like popsicle sticks, used for mixing resin, adhesive etc.

## GLUE BRUSHES

These are short-handled paintbrushes used for applying multipurpose white (PVA) glue and varnish.

## HAMMER

A standard ball-pein or claw hammer in a medium size is all you need for tapping letter punches.

## STEEL BLOCK

A steel block is used when hammering or letter punching as a solid support for the metal you are working on.

## TAPE MEASURE

A tape measure is an essential tool for measuring chain, wire, and fabric for your designs.

STEEL BLOCK

MIXING STICKS

GLUE BRUSH

HAMMER

TAPE MEASURE

# Materials

THE PROJECTS IN THIS BOOK COVER A WIDE RANGE OF CRAFTS TO ALLOW YOU TO CREATE STRIKING BIRD-THEMED ACCESSORIES. YOU WILL NEED A GOOD SELECTION OF DIFFERENT MATERIALS TO PRODUCE YOUR DESIGNS.

## CHARMS

A charm is a small ornament you can attach to jewelry and accessories. You can buy traditional metal charms or make your own by using items such as buttons, feathers, and washers.

## BEADS

Beads are available in all colors, shapes, sizes, and materials. You can create entire pieces with beads or use them to add detail, color, and interest to your designs.

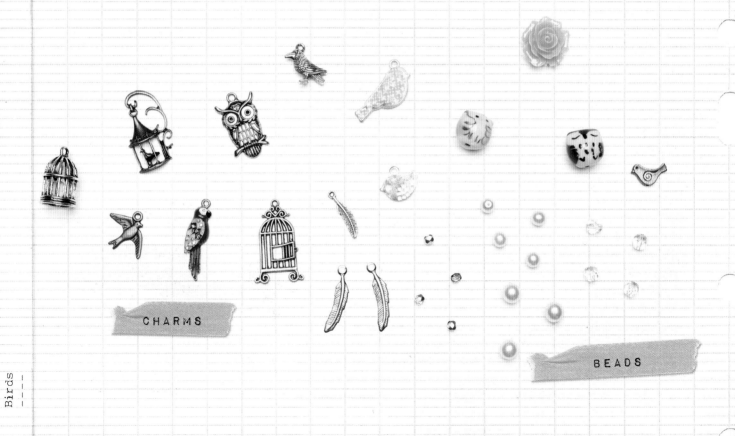

CHARMS

BEADS

## PAPER

Collect beautiful wrapping paper, images from books and magazines, and old sheet music to use for collage and decoupage or as inspiration for your designs.

## SHRINK PLASTIC

You can print and draw on this amazing plastic sheet and cut it into shapes. When baked in the oven it shrinks up to 50 percent and becomes a hard plastic.

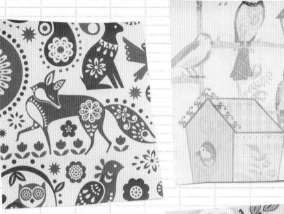

PAPER

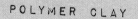

SHRINK PLASTIC

POLYMER CLAY

## POLYMER CLAY

This modeling clay is hardened by baking in the oven. There are various brands available and all are suitable for molds and modeling by hand.

## FABRICS

You only need small amounts of fabric to make accessories. Look around thrift stores for interesting fabrics, or buy scraps as a cheap option. Felt is useful and can be bought cheaply in small colorful squares.

## WIRE

Craft wire is commonly base metal such as copper and bronze and also silver- or gold-plated. It is available in various thicknesses, usually in a coil or on a reel.

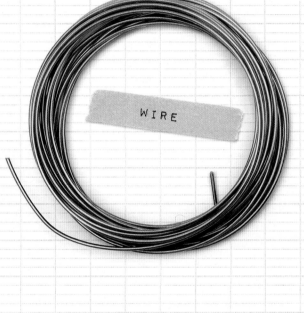

FABRICS

WIRE

CHAIN

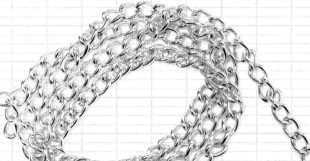

## CHAIN

There are many types, sizes, and finishes of chain available. Make sure that the chain is strong enough to hold an item but not so heavy that it overpowers the design.

# findings

Findings are all the little components used in jewelry making, and other crafts, to manufacture or assemble your accessories. There is a huge variety of findings available from craft or bead stores and online sources, but here are a few you will find useful for the projects in this book.

## JUMPRINGS

A jumpring is a single loop of wire that comes in different sizes and thicknesses. It is used to connect findings and jewelry together or to join or attach charms.

## HEADPINS / EYEPINS

These are lengths of wire about 2in (5cm) long with either a small open loop or a pinhead at one end. They are used to connect beads and charms together or onto other components.

## EARRINGS

There are different types available, such as fish hook and kidney-shape ear wires, and different-size hoops from which you can hang charms, chain, or beads.

## BROOCH BAR

These are available in different lengths. Each consists of a simple hinged pin fitting that can be glued or sewn onto your designs.

## BEZELS

A bezel setting has a flat back with a metal rim around the edge designed to surround a gemstone or cabochon. Bezels are perfect for holding an image coated with epoxy resin and exist as rings, earrings, pendants, or just plain.

## CUFFLINK BACKS

These hold the edges of the cuff together. Each cufflink back has a small flat disk to enable it to be easily glued onto your designs.

## LOBSTER CATCHES

A clasp commonly used opposite a jumpring to fasten necklaces and bracelets. The catch is opened by pulling back the tiny trigger.

EARRINGS

BROOCH BAR

BEZEL

CUFFLINK BACKS

EYEPIN

JUMPRINGS

LOBSTER CATCHES

Materials

# adhesives and topcoats

### WHITE (PVA) GLUE

This is multipurpose glue for use with paper, fabric, and wood. It dries clear and so is also an excellent sealant for paper being used with resin or as decoupage.

### EPOXY ADHESIVE

This two-part extra strong adhesive bonds many materials, including metal, ceramics, and wood, and is the best glue for attaching metal findings to your designs.

### HOT-MELT ADHESIVE (HOT GLUE)

The glue comes in solid sticks that you insert into an electric glue gun and melts as the gun heats. It is sticky when hot, sets very quickly, and is useful for many crafts.

### CLEAR DIMENSIONAL ADHESIVE

This dries to a crystal clear finish and is good for gluing glass cabochons. It can also be used as a paper sealant, a glasslike topcoat, or to stop the ends of ribbon from fraying.

### VARNISH

Clear polyurethane that creates a tough protective topcoat for paper decoupage, wood, or beads.

### SUPERGLUE

A fast-acting adhesive that binds a range of materials.

CLEAR DIMENSIONAL ADHESIVE

EPOXY ADHESIVE

WHITE (PVA) GLUE

GLUE GUN STICKS

VARNISH

GLUE GUN

SUPERGLUE

# threads

## COTTON POLYESTER

This is the most commonly used all-purpose thread and is suitable for all of the projects in this book. A strong thread, it is available in a huge range of colors.

## EMBROIDERY FLOSS

This is usually six strands of twisted thread made from cotton, silk, or rayon. The strands can be untwisted and separated and are ideal for securing or creating decorative features in your work.

## INVISIBLE THREAD

This nylon thread is great for using when you don't want your stitching to be seen.

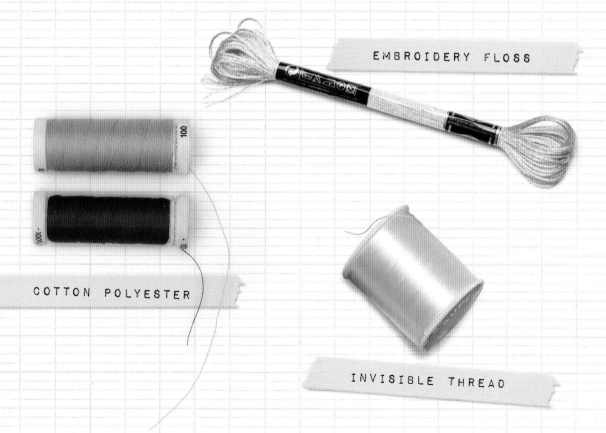

EMBROIDERY FLOSS

COTTON POLYESTER

INVISIBLE THREAD

# Basic techniques

ALL OF THE TECHNIQUES USED IN THIS BOOK CAN BE MASTERED WITH JUST A LITTLE PRACTISE. FOLLOW THESE STEP-BY-STEP PHOTOGRAPHIC INSTRUCTIONS AND YOU'LL BE AMAZED AT HOW EASY IT IS TO CREATE THESE STUNNING PROJECTS.

## jumprings

These are available to buy ready-made in various sizes, thicknesses, and colors; the larger the quantity you buy, the more economical they will be.

### OPENING AND CLOSING JUMPRINGS

It is important to know how to open and close jumprings without destroying their shape.

1 Take two pairs of pliers (flat- or snipe-nose work well) and hold one pair in each hand.

2 Grip both sides of the jumpring, keeping the opening in the center at the top.

3 Gently move the left-hand pliers away from you and the right-hand pliers toward you. This will open the jumpring while keeping the circular shape intact. To close the jumpring, reverse the technique until the ends meet and are flush against one another.

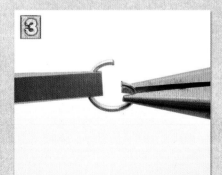

# headpins

Headpins are a single length of wire with a tiny pinhead at one end. They act as a stopper for beads threaded onto the wire. Headpins are used to attach beads to chain, findings, or other beads.

## WRAPPED LOOP IN A HEADPIN

This is a loop made in a headpin after a bead has been threaded on.

1 Thread a bead onto a headpin. Ensure it goes all the way down the shaft and that the pinhead is flush with the bead.

2 Bend the length of wire back against the bead to a 90-degree angle. Keep the head or loop of the pin flush with the bead.

3 Grip the bent wire with round-nose pliers just beyond the bend. With your other hand, pull the end of the wire back around the tip of the pliers. Go all the way around and make a loop until the wire points in the other direction.

4 Thread the finding along the wire and into the loop, so that you close the wrapped loop with the item attached.

5 Hold the top of the loop with snipe-nose pliers and, holding onto the end of the wire with your other hand, wrap it around the wire below the loop until it forms a spiral on top of the bead.

6 Using side or end cutters, snip off the remaining wire close to the end of the spiral. Using the tip of the snipe-nose pliers, push the cut end of the wire in against the spiral to prevent a sharp edge. You may need to straighten the loop with round-nose pliers.

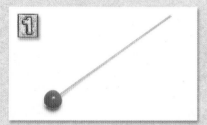

Basic techniques

# shrink plastic

This amazing plastic sheet shrinks to 50 percent of its original size when baked in the oven and becomes a strong plastic shape. You can cut it into any shape, color it, paint it, stamp onto it with inks, and print images onto it.

## HOW TO USE SHRINK PLASTIC

Regular shrink film is fine for most methods and comes in black and matte as well. Buy special Inkjet shrink film for printing images from the computer (this comes in white and clear).

1 If you will be coloring the plastic, sand the surface with medium-weight sandpaper in a crisscross pattern.

2 Trace, draw, or print your design onto the shrink plastic 50 percent bigger than you want it to be. Cut it out with scissors and use a hole punch to make any holes that you need.

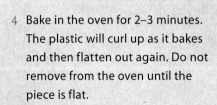

3 Preheat your oven to 350–400°F (180–200°C). Line a baking sheet with parchment paper (baking paper), place your plastic designs on it, and cover them with another piece of parchment paper.

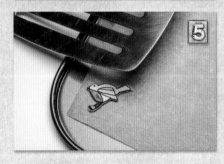

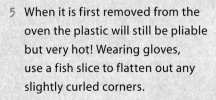

4 Bake in the oven for 2–3 minutes. The plastic will curl up as it bakes and then flatten out again. Do not remove from the oven until the piece is flat.

5 When it is first removed from the oven the plastic will still be pliable but very hot! Wearing gloves, use a fish slice to flatten out any slightly curled corners.

# metal stamping

This is the process of imprinting letters, numbers, or motifs by hand onto metal using steel punches and a hammer. Metal stamping is an excellent technique for personalizing your designs.

## HOW TO USE LETTER PUNCHES ON METAL

Letter punches are available in upper or lower case, various fonts, and different sizes. The charm of hand-stamped words is the quirky look you get from the imperfect spacing of the letters.

1 Place your jeweler's steel block onto a solid surface and place the metal blank with the side you want to punch on facing up.

2 If you are stamping in a straight line, put masking tape along the metal blank underneath where you want to stamp and write each letter. You can then follow this line for each stamp.

3 If you are stamping onto a washer or round blank, put a dot in marker pen where you want each letter to be. You can line up the stamp and then rub off the pen marks with denatured alcohol (methylated spirit) afterward.

4 The letter of each stamp is engraved into the side of it so you can see which way it faces. Take the first stamp, with the letter on the side facing you, and position it.

5 Hold the stamp firmly and straight, and hit the top end once with a hammer blow. An impression of the letter will appear in the metal. Repeat for all the letters.

# epoxy resin

Epoxy resin is used in jewelry making to simulate a clear liquid. It starts off with two separate liquids which, when mixed together, trigger a chemical reaction that results in a hard plastic or strong adhesive. Resin can be used to cast entire objects or as a thick topcoat for your jewelry pieces. Both produce amazing results and give a professional finish to your craft projects.

## HOW TO MIX EPOXY RESIN AND FILL A BEZEL

Two-part epoxy resin, such as Envirotex Lite, is very easy to use, especially as it is designed to degas itself so most bubbles will rise to the surface and pop. It is perfect for pouring into bezels covering decorative images or bits and pieces—almost like creating your own gemstones!

1 Ensure you are in a well-ventilated room. Cover the surface you are working on to protect it from any drips, get two flat-sided plastic cups and a wooden mixing stick ready, and wear protective gloves.

2 Pour the required amount of resin into one of the plastic cups and then pour EXACTLY the same amount of hardener into the other plastic cup. It is important that you use the same amount of resin and hardener or the adhesive may not set properly.

3 Pour all of the resin into the cup with the hardener and mix vigorously with the wooden mixing stick for 1 minute. Use the mixing stick to scrape the sides and bring up the fluid from the bottom of the cup so it all gets blended.

**5** Now the mixture is ready to go into the bezel on top of the image that has been sealed with white glue (PVA). Use the mixing stick to pick up a small blob of it and let it drip into the bezel. Keep repeating this until the bezel is full, but do not allow the resin to leak over the edge.

**6** Leave for 5 minutes, then remove the tiny bubbles. Take a straw and very gently exhale evenly over the surface where the bubbles are until they disappear. Keep checking every so often so if any new bubbles appear you can pop them with a toothpick.

**4** Pour this mixture back into the plastic cup that had the resin in, using the mixing stick to scrape all of it out, and mix again vigorously for another minute. It will look frothy and full of bubbles.

**7** Make sure your bezel is on a flat surface, cover it with a plastic container to protect from dust, and leave to cure (harden). You should be able to handle your piece in 24 hours but it will take 72 hours for it to completely cure.

Basic techniques

# epoxy adhesive

One advantage to epoxy adhesive is that it has a long working time, meaning that parts can be repositioned for up to 90 minutes. When it does set it is extremely strong and no other adhesive is as good as this for gluing metal findings to your designs.

## HOW TO MIX EPOXY ADHESIVE

1 Squeeze equal amounts of the resin and hardener next to each other onto a clean disposable surface such as a piece of paper or cardboard.

2 Using a mixing stick, scrape the resin and hardener together into the middle and mix thoroughly for at least 30 seconds until they are well mixed.

3 Make sure both of the surfaces you will be gluing are clean and dry, and for ultimate bonding slightly sand both surfaces. Apply the adhesive to both surfaces and glue together.

4 Ensure your piece is on a flat surface or is balanced so that it stays in position while the adhesive dries. It will be ready to handle after 8 hours but won't be fully hardened for 14 hours.

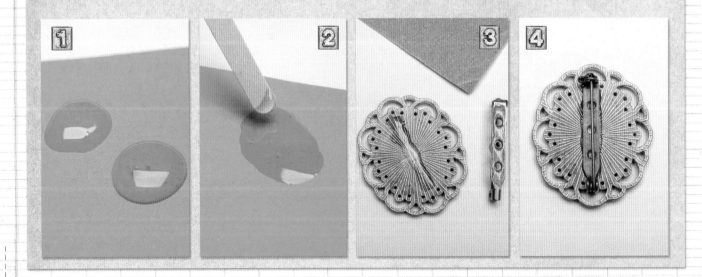

# double-sided fabric adhesive

This is a double-sided adhesive web with a paper backing that bonds fabrics together when ironed. It is available by the yard or meter and is a handy alternative to sewing that can be used on most kinds of fabric.

## HOW TO USE DOUBLE-SIDED FABRIC ADHESIVE

Run your fingers over the rough adhesive side so you know how it feels. This will help later when you need to make sure you don't iron the wrong side.

1 Draw or trace your shape onto the smooth paper side of the adhesive. If it's a shape that needs to come out the right way around, draw it backward.

2 Cut out the shape in the fabric adhesive.

3 Place the fabric that you want the shape to be cut out of on the ironing board with the wrong side up. Lay the fabric adhesive onto the fabric with the paper side on top.

4 With the iron on the cotton setting, iron the fabric adhesive to the fabric using a firm pressing technique. It should take about 10 seconds.

5 Leave to cool, then neatly cut around the finished shape. Carefully peel off the paper backing to reveal the adhesive coating.

6 Put the fabric ready for sticking the shape on onto the ironing board, right side up. Place the shape adhesive-side down on top of the fabric and iron over it so it sticks. Leave the pieces to cool flat for about 20 minutes.

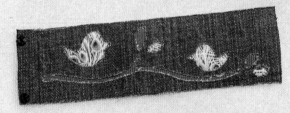

# sewing

Basic hand-sewing techniques are used in a lot of projects, either to create a form by sewing pieces of fabric together or to close gaps, attach findings, or simply to create an attractive decoration.

## RUNNING STITCH

This is the most basic stitch and is easy to use for many aspects in your projects. If the stitches will be visible, try to keep them all the same length.

1   Push your threaded needle up through the fabric from the back to the front and pull until you reach the knot at the end of the thread.

2   Push the needle back down through the fabric in line with where it just came up and pull the thread through. The space you leave between these two points determines the length of your stitch.

3   Now push the needle back up through the fabric leaving a space from the previous stitch, and back down to create your second stitch. Continue like this until you have the number of stitches you require.

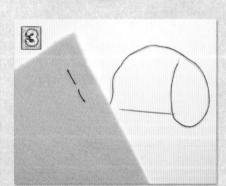

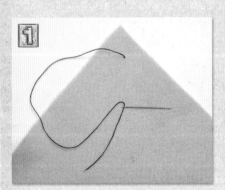
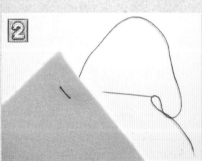

## BACKSTITCH

This is like running stitch but is used to create strong seams in a similar way to a sewing machine.

1. Start off with one running stitch. Push the needle back up through the fabric, pulling the thread all the way through, leaving a space from the first stitch.

2. Push your needle back down though the fabric at the end of the first stitch, pulling the thread all the way through. This is the 'back' part referred to in backstitch.

3. Now push your needle back up through the fabric a space away from the previous stitch and repeat step 2. And that's it! Keep repeating until you have all the stitches you need.

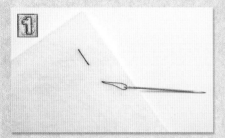

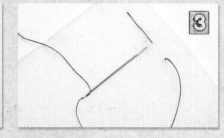

## WHIPSTITCH

This is a simple looping stitch that can be used to create a seam in two pieces of fabric.

1. Push your threaded needle up through both of the fabrics you are joining and pull the thread through until you reach the knot in the end of the thread.

2. Now take your needle over the edge and push through the back of the fabrics again and out through the front next to the original stitch.

3. Keep going like this, keeping the stitches close together to create a strong seam.

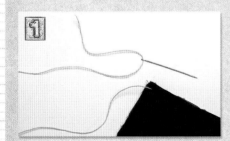
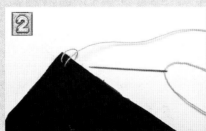
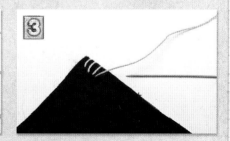

Basic techniques

**earrings**

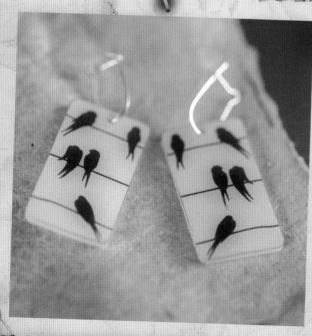

# feathery

This project is ideal for using up charms from old broken earrings you have lying around and giving them a new lease of life!

# Everything you will need...

Try to use matching size and shape feathers for each pair of earrings as it creates a nice balanced look.

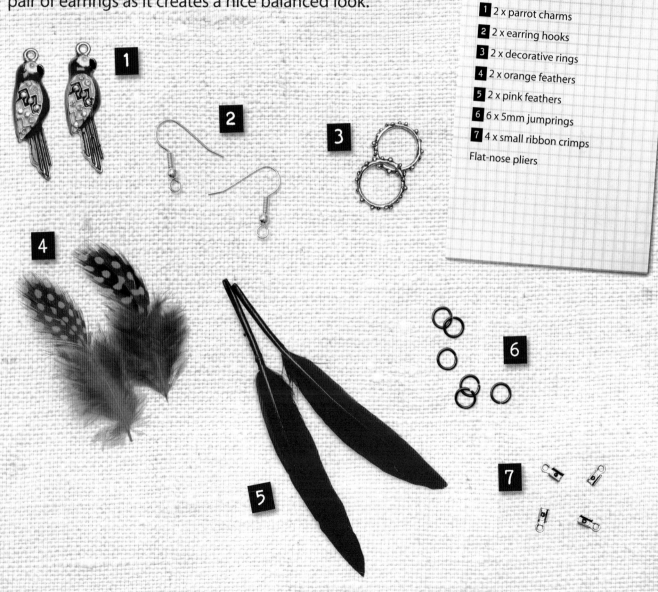

1. 2 x parrot charms
2. 2 x earring hooks
3. 2 x decorative rings
4. 2 x orange feathers
5. 2 x pink feathers
6. 6 x 5mm jumprings
7. 4 x small ribbon crimps

Flat-nose pliers

feathery

# Assembling the earrings

**1** Using the pliers, grip the loop on the earring hook and twist your hand away from yourself to open the loop without distorting it.

**2** Place the decorative ring into the open loop and then close the loop again with the pliers.

**3** Open a 5mm jumpring (see page 18) and thread the parrot charm onto it. Thread this through the loop at the bottom of the earring hook and close the jumpring.

**4** Place the stalk of the pink feather into the cord crimp and, using your pliers, firmly flatten the left side down and then the right side on top of it to secure the feather. Repeat this with the other three feathers.

**5** Open four of the 5mm jumprings and thread the feathers onto them. Do not close the jumprings.

**6** Attach the jumpring with the orange feather to the bottom of the decorative ring and the jumpring with the pink feather to the right of it. Repeat the process to make the second earring.

FOR MAXIMUM
IMPACT, TRY A
LARGER DECORATIVE
RING OR HOOP AND
MORE FEATHERS.

feathery

# songbird

Take inspiration from the huge
trend for decorative birdcages,
and create these enchanting
miniatures to be worn
as earrings.

# Everything you will need...

Use feather charms for this project or you could use two different bird charms.

**1** 0.8mm (SWG 21, AWG 20) wire
**2** 0.3mm (SWG 30, AWG 28) wire
**3** 2 x 7mm jumprings
**4** 2 x earring hooks
**5** 2 x feather charms
Cutters
Pen
Round-nose pliers
Glue gun and glue sticks
Flat-nose pliers

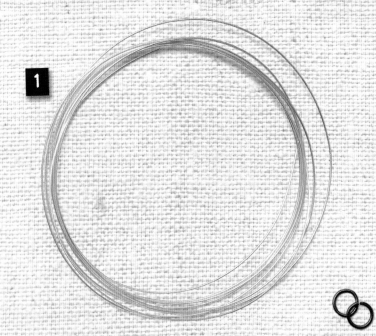

**1**

**3**

**2**

**4**

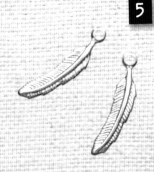

**5**

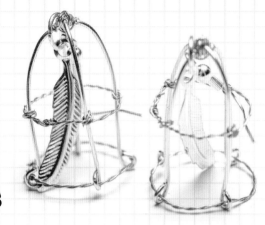

# Assembling the earrings

1 Using the cutters, cut four pieces of 0.8mm wire to 3in (7.5cm) long. Bend each wire in half over a pen to form an arch shape. Then, using round-nose pliers, grip the very ends of the wire with the tips of the pliers and turn 180 degrees to form a tiny closed loop on each end.

2 Place one arch on top of the other to form a cross. Lift the top arch away and put a blob of hot glue on the center of the arch below. Replace the top arch and press together. Repeat with the other two arches.

3 Next, use your fingers to wrap some 0.3mm wire around the glued joint of the arches and pull the end of the wire tightly with the pliers to fully secure the structure.

4 Using the cutters, cut four pieces of 0.3mm wire to 3in (7.5cm). Twist two pieces together tightly and then form into a circle shape, but don't secure the ends. Repeat with the other two pieces of wire.

5 Thread the twisted wire circle through all four of the loops at the ends of the wire arches of one birdcage. Now secure the ends of the wire circle by twisting them around each other twice. Repeat with the second birdcage.

6 Repeat step 4 but cut the wire to 2$\frac{1}{2}$in (6cm) and secure the ends of the circles this time. Then slide them over the top of the wire arches until they reach halfway down.

7 Wrap 0.3mm wire around each of the four points that the circle crosses the arches, to secure the whole cage. Do this on both cages.

8 Open a 7mm jumpring widely (see page 18) and thread through the loop of the earring hook. Next, thread on the feather charm and then thread through the top of the birdcage directly across the join at the top. Close the jumpring so the earring is complete. Repeat on the second birdcage.

FOR A DESIGN TWIST, HANG TWO DIFFERENT CHARMS INSIDE THE CAGES— FOR EXAMPLE, A GOLD STAR IN ONE AND A HEART IN THE OTHER.

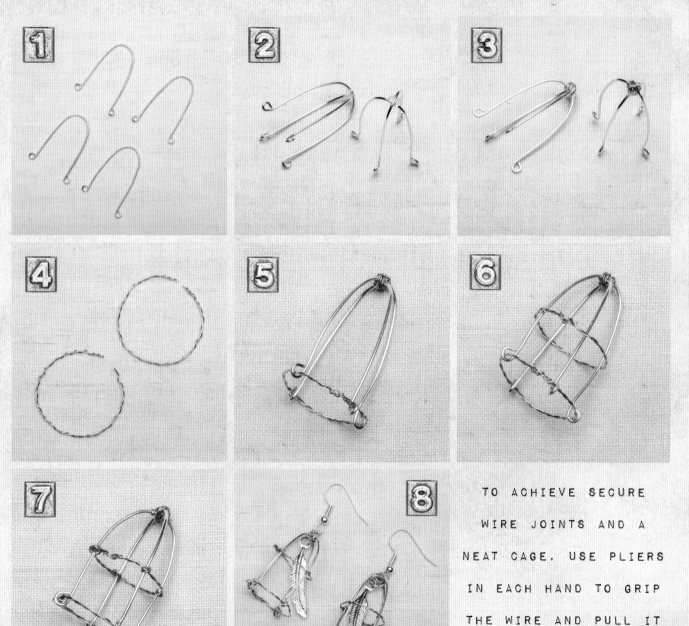

TO ACHIEVE SECURE
WIRE JOINTS AND A
NEAT CAGE, USE PLIERS
IN EACH HAND TO GRIP
THE WIRE AND PULL IT
TIGHT WHEN WRAPPING
IT AROUND THE JOINTS.

songbird

# silhouette

The silhouette of a bird on a
wire is a timeless and beautiful
motif that works perfectly on
these simple earrings.

# Everything you will need...

This shrink plastic is specially coated for use with Inkjet printers, so all you need to do is decide on your image, print it out, and you'll have a flawless design ready to use.

**1** Birds on wire template

**2** 2 x earring hooks

**3** Clear Inkjet shrink plastic

Clear dimensional adhesive, such as Diamond Glaze

Inkjet printer

Scissors

Hole punch

Parchment paper (baking paper)

Baking sheet

Glue brush

**1**

**3**

**2**

# Assembling the earrings

**1** Scan in the two earring templates (see page 39) and print out onto the correct side of the shrink plastic. Leave the ink to dry for a few minutes before handling.

**2** Cut the designs out of the sheet by following the rectangular outline of each template.

**3** Using a hole punch, carefully punch one hole in the top center of each piece of plastic.

**4** Place the pieces of plastic on a sheet of parchment paper. Put on a baking sheet and bake in the oven for 2–3 minutes (see page 20).

**5** When shrunk, remove from the oven and leave to cool. To seal your printed design, use a glue brush to coat the pieces of plastic with a thin layer of clear dimensional adhesive.

**6** Take one earring hook, open it, and thread the shrink plastic onto it until it rests in the groove at the front. Repeat with the other earring hook.

TO FIND THE PRINT SIDE OF SHRINK PLASTIC, PRESS A SLIGHTLY WET FINGER ONTO A CORNER OF BOTH SIDES. THE DULL, STICKY SIDE IS THE SIDE TO PRINT ONTO.

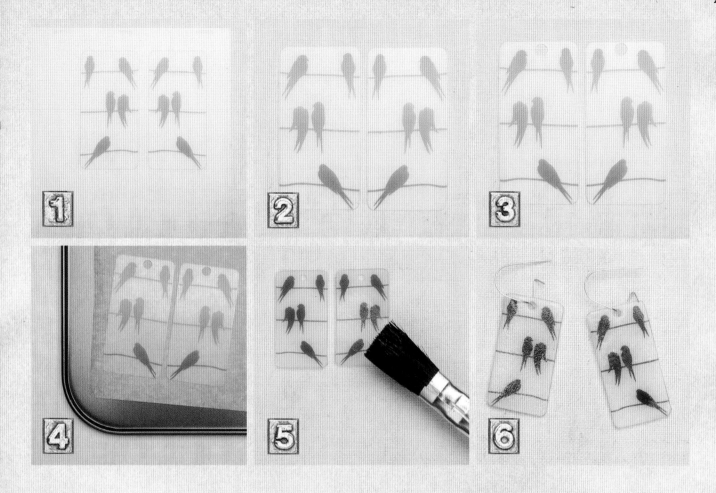

AS THE PLASTIC SHRINKS THE COLORS INTENSIFY,
SO EITHER REDUCE THE COLOR INTENSITY ON YOUR PRINTER
SETTINGS OR REDUCE THE OPACITY OF YOUR DESIGN
TO 50% IF CREATING IT ON A COMPUTER.

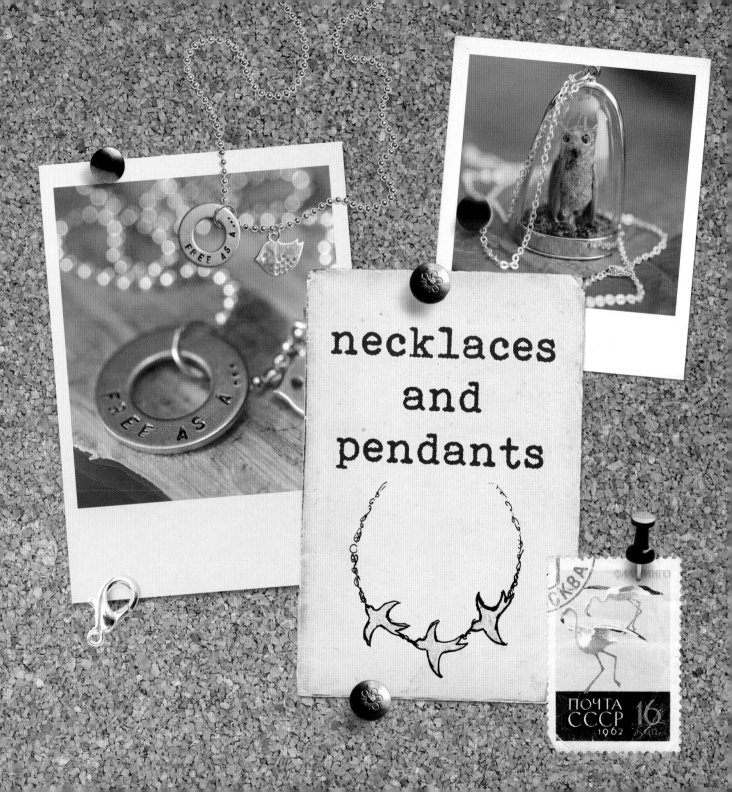

# necklaces
# and
# pendants

# flight

Keep your look bold, simple,
and bang on trend with this
fashionable laser-cut necklace.

# Everything you will need...

Laser cutting is affordable and allows you to create 3D accessories from your 2D drawings with minimum fuss.

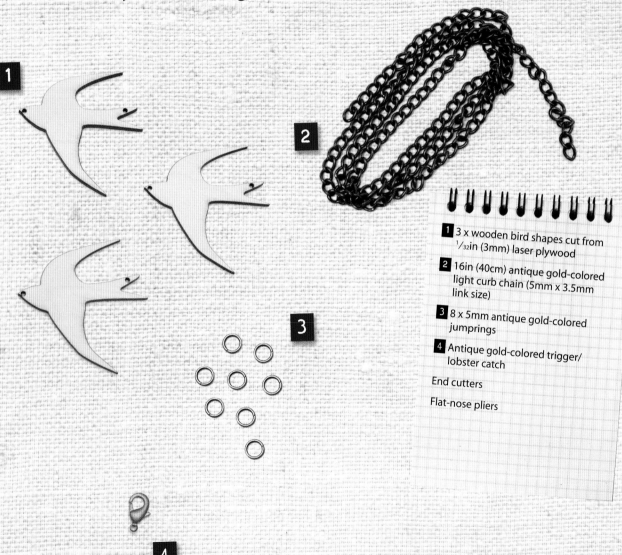

**1** 3 x wooden bird shapes cut from ¹/₃₂in (3mm) laser plywood

**2** 16in (40cm) antique gold-colored light curb chain (5mm x 3.5mm link size)

**3** 8 x 5mm antique gold-colored jumprings

**4** Antique gold-colored trigger/lobster catch

End cutters

Flat-nose pliers

flight

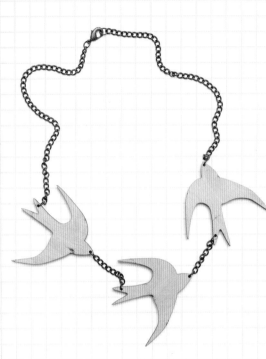

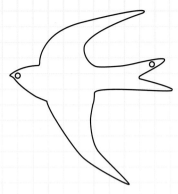

# Assembling the necklace

**1** Using the end cutters, cut two pieces of chain measuring 5¼in (13cm) each and two pieces of chain measuring 1in (2.5cm) each.

**2** Put your three wooden birds in a line, all facing the same direction and the same way up. Place one piece of long chain in front of the first bird, the other long chain after the last bird, and the two short pieces of chain in between the three birds. This is the layout of your necklace.

**3** Open a 5mm jumpring (see page 18), thread it through the hole in the tail of the first bird, through the end of the chain next to it, and then close it.

**4** Repeat step 3 but thread the jumpring through the nose of the same bird and the chain next to it.

**5** Repeat steps 3 and 4 with the other two birds and the remaining chains.

**6** Open a 5mm jumpring and thread through one end of the long chain and close. Then open the last 5mm jumpring, thread though the end of the other long chain, thread the trigger catch onto it, and close.

YOU CAN ALSO LASER-CUT OR ENGRAVE PLASTICS, LEATHER, FABRIC, PAPER, METALS, MIRRORS, AND CERAMICS.

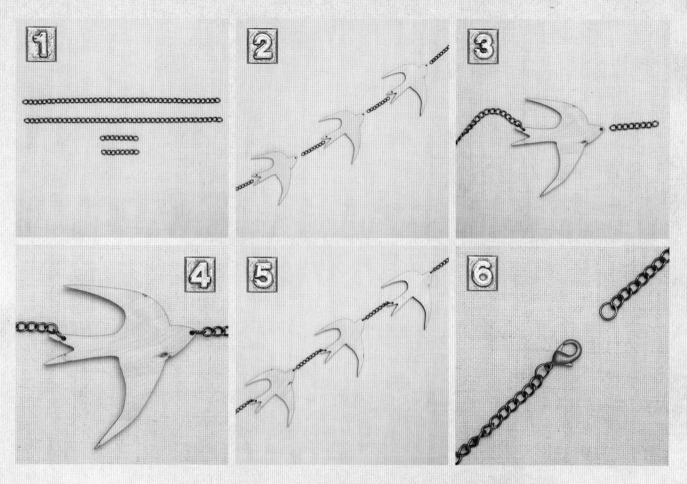

DON'T BE PUT OFF BY LASER-CUTTING
STORES ASKING FOR TECHNICAL DRAWINGS
PRODUCED ON A COMPUTER. MOST ARE
ALSO HAPPY TO WORK FROM A SIMPLE
HAND-DRAWN IMAGE.

# beady

Liven up your outfit by adding this
striking chunky bead necklace.

# Everything you will need...

It is best to use fabric patterned with small birds to show off the design on each bead.

1 4in x 23²/₃in (10cm x 60cm) fabric strip, with a bird pattern

2 8 x 1in (25mm) wooden beads

3 Silver embroidery floss

4 40in (1.02m) ribbon

5 Reel of cotton to match your fabric

Fabric scissors

Sewing machine

Pin

Needle

Lighter

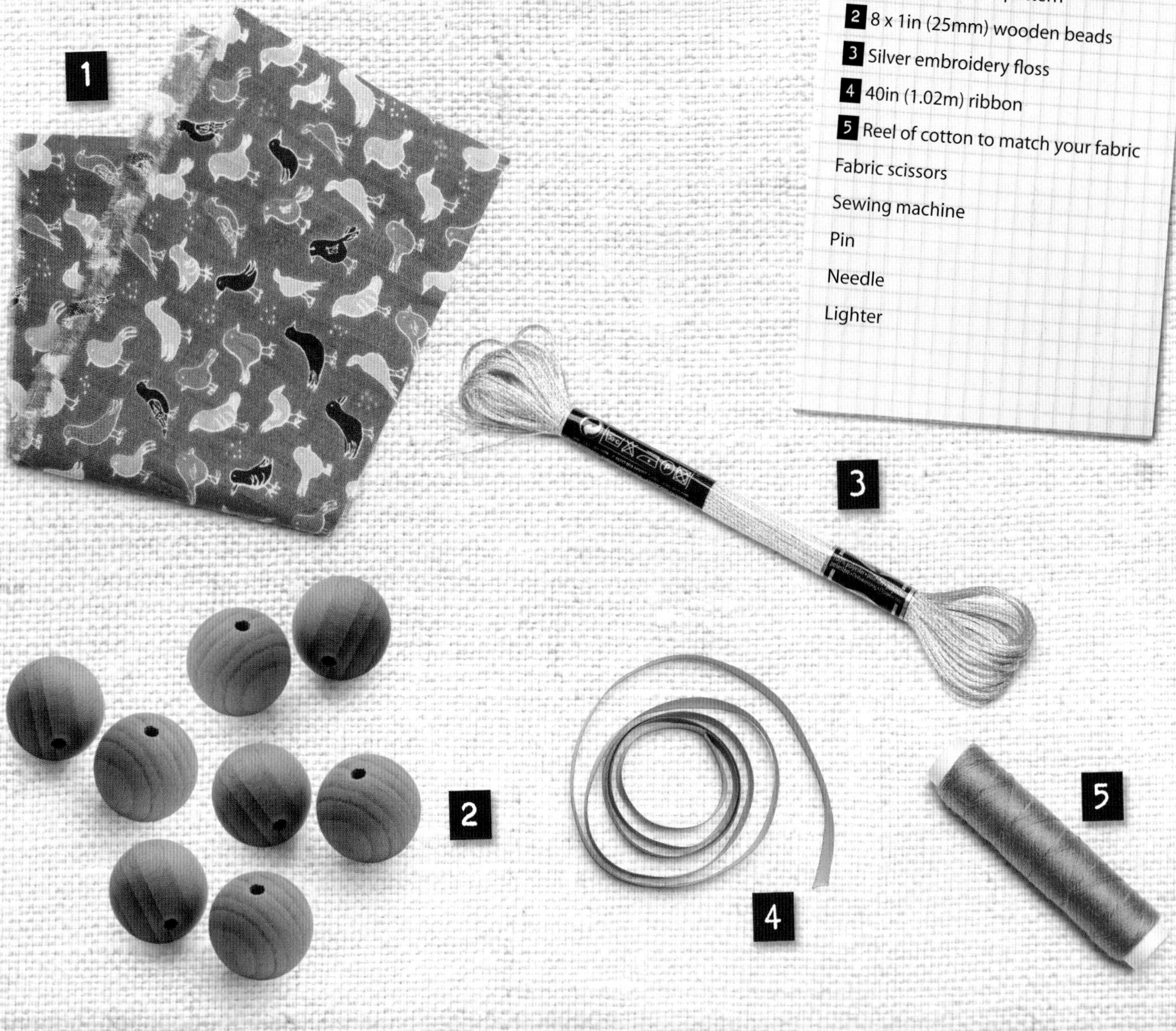

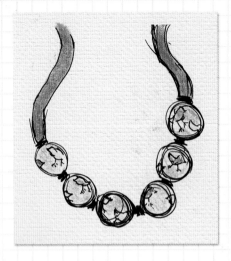

# Assembling the necklace

**1** To determine the width of your fabric strip, wrap it around one of the beads and then measure how much was used. Then add ⅝in (1.5cm) for the seam allowance and room to slide the beads in. Cut the strip.

**2** Turn the strip over so the pattern is facing right side up and fold the strip in half lengthways. Machine stitch all the way along the open edge (opposite side to the fold), leaving just over a ¼in (5mm) seam allowance. Leave the two ends open.

**3** Turn the tube of fabric inside out, so that the pattern is now showing. Fold the tube in half to find the middle and thread a pin into that point.

**4** Slide a bead into the tube until it reaches the pin. Thread a needle with approximately 32in (81cm) of the embroidery floss, knot the end, and sew through the tube as close to the side of the bead as possible. Wrap the floss around the tube tightly several times, leaving enough to sew back through the tube and tie a knot. Trim the end neatly.

**5** Remove the pin from the other side of the bead and repeat step 4.

**6** Continue to add beads in the same way until you have six beads in the tube.

**7** Slide in one more bead and make sure you have enough material to cover it and leave a hem allowance of ¼in (5mm). Cut off the excess material and fold the hem over.

**8** Cut two pieces of ribbon to 17½in (45cm) and melt the ends slightly with a lighter to prevent fraying. Put one end in the tube with the bead and stitch to one side of the material with the teal thread.

**9** Sew running stitch with thread all around the top of the tube and then pull on the cotton to gather the ends in together. Continue to stitch until the end is closed securely. Repeat steps 7 to 9 with the other end of the tube.

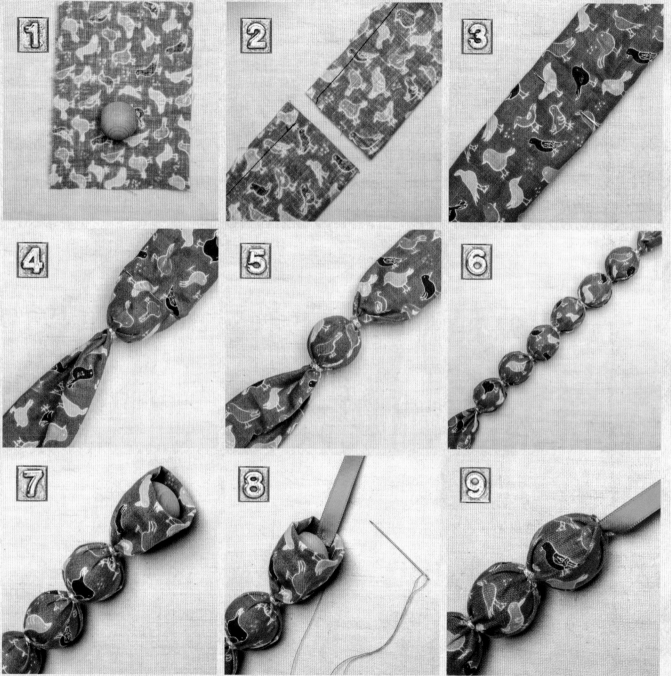

# stamp

Make a statement with this letter-stamped pendant! The slightly imperfect alignment of letters adds to its rustic, handmade charm.

# Everything you will need...

Using washers from hardware stores is a cheap and easy option—there are different sizes and metals available.

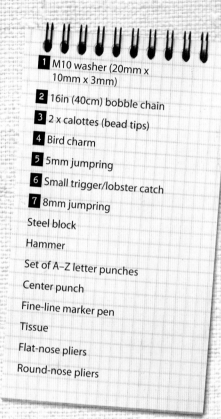

1 M10 washer (20mm x 10mm x 3mm)

2 16in (40cm) bobble chain

3 2 x calottes (bead tips)

4 Bird charm

5 5mm jumpring

6 Small trigger/lobster catch

7 8mm jumpring

Steel block

Hammer

Set of A–Z letter punches

Center punch

Fine-line marker pen

Tissue

Flat-nose pliers

Round-nose pliers

stamp

# Assembling the necklace

1 Take your washer and place it onto a steel block on a flat solid surface, such as the floor, that will not move when hammered on. If you don't have a steel block just place straight onto the solid surface.

2 Using your letter punches, hammer each letter of your phrase onto the washer (see page 21). Stamp the letters so they follow the curve of the washer. Hammer a center punch the same way as the letters, to stamp three dots after the last word.

3 Color inside each letter with a fine-line marker pen and then wipe away the excess marker pen with a tissue. The black should stay inside the letters.

4 Place the end ball of your chain into a calotte and use flat-nose pliers to squeeze both sides to close the calotte around the ball tightly. Repeat on the other end of the chain.

5 Put one jaw of the round-nose pliers through the loop on the calotte and bend it around to create a closed loop. Do this to both calottes.

6 Open a 5mm jumpring (see page 18). Thread the lobster catch onto it, then thread through the loop in the calotte at one end of the chain and close the jumpring. Open another 5mm jumpring and attach through the calotte at the other end of the chain.

7 Open the 8mm jumpring and slide the washer onto it, then open the 5mm jumpring and thread the bird charm onto it.

8 Position the 8mm jumpring with the washer around the ball chain and close to attach. Attach the 5mm jumpring with the bird to the right of the washer.

USE LETTER AND NUMBER PUNCHES ON CHARMS OR TAGS TO PERSONALIZE YOUR DESIGNS WITH NAMES, DATES, OR ABSOLUTELY ANYTHING YOU FANCY!

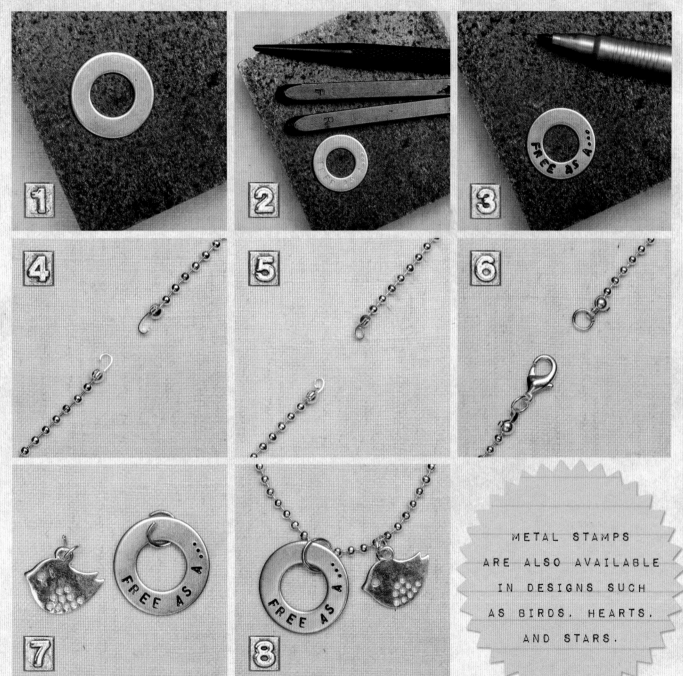

METAL STAMPS ARE ALSO AVAILABLE IN DESIGNS SUCH AS BIRDS, HEARTS, AND STARS.

stamp

# wisdom

Using faux taxidermy is a huge trend in the designer jewelry world. Make your own fake with this cute owl locket pendant.

# Everything you will need...

Dolls' house items and miniature animals can also be used to help you create imaginative scenes inside a locket.

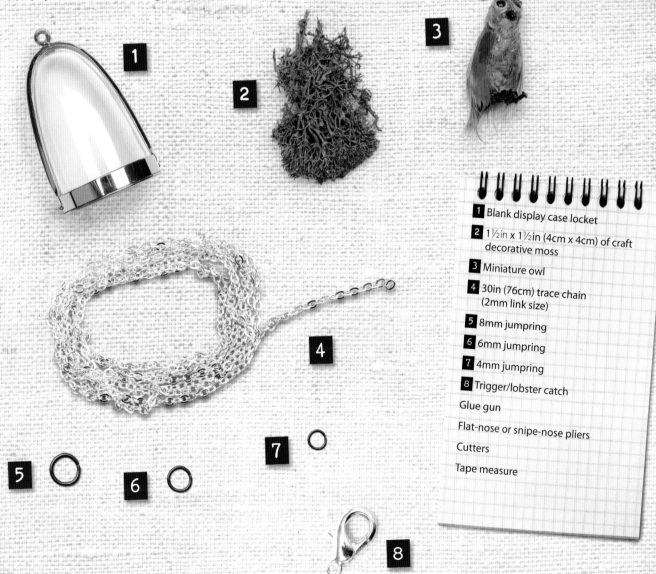

1 Blank display case locket

2 1½in x 1½in (4cm x 4cm) of craft decorative moss

3 Miniature owl

4 30in (76cm) trace chain (2mm link size)

5 8mm jumpring

6 6mm jumpring

7 4mm jumpring

8 Trigger/lobster catch

Glue gun

Flat-nose or snipe-nose pliers

Cutters

Tape measure

WHATEVER COLOR LOCKET YOU USE,
BE SURE TO CHOOSE CHAIN AND
FINDINGS TO MATCH IT.

# Assembling the pendant

1 Remove the pin that secures the base of the locket and lift the top off.

2 Break off a small piece of moss, just enough to just cover most of the base of the locket but not to spill over the edges. Cover the base of the locket with hot glue and quickly press and hold the moss on top of it.

3 Cover the bottom of the owl and his feet in hot glue and quickly stick him on top of the moss in the center of the locket base.

4 Ensure all glue is dry and the owl is secure, and then replace the top of the locket and push the pin back through the base to secure.

5 Using the pliers, open a 8mm jumpring (see page 18), thread through the loop at the top of the locket and close.

6 Open a 4mm jumpring, thread the trigger catch onto it, and attach to one end of the chain.

7 Thread the end of the chain without the catch through the 8mm jumpring at the top of the locket and pull through to halfway along. Open a 6mm jumpring and attach to the end of the chain without the trigger catch and close.

IF THE MOSS IS LOOSE AFTER YOU HAVE STUCK DOWN THE OWL, GENTLY LIFT IT, AND PUT ANOTHER BLOB OF HOT GLUE UNDERNEATH.

bracelets,
bangles,
and rings

# decoupage

Decoupage (decorating a surface
with paper cutouts) is a great way
to incorporate bird illustrations
into your designs.

# Everything you will need...

This is the perfect project to revamp your old bangles, but you can also buy blank bangles in wood or plastic in any size or style you desire.

1. 3 x different sheets of standard size wrapping paper with bird motifs
2. White (PVA) glue
3. Bangle
4. Clear varnish

Scissors

Tape measure

Glue brush

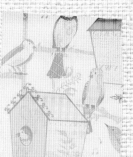

**1**

**3**

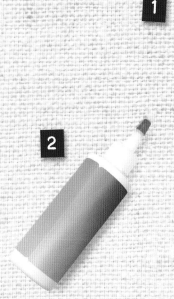

**2**

**4**

decoupage

# Assembling the bangle

**1** Cut out squares of $1\frac{1}{4}$in x $1\frac{1}{4}$in (3cm x 3cm), and smaller, of bird images from different wrapping papers. Also cut some thinner strips and rectangles, no longer than 2in (5cm), of other patterns from the wrapping paper to fill in the gaps between the birds.

**2** Take the first square of wrapping paper and brush a generous amount of glue all over the back of it.

**3** Stick the paper onto the bangle. Then apply a generous amount of glue to your brush and cover the front of the image completely, going over the edges onto the bangle.

**4** Add another two pieces of wrapping paper to the bangle and stick down using the glue. Use your finger to smooth the paper down flat and push out any wrinkles. Make sure that all of the paper is stuck to the bangle.

**5** Overlap the edges of the bangle with the bird images and fold them around so they stick to the inside. This makes a neat edge and continues the decoration so no gaps show through at all.

**6** Keep adding images and glue as above, slightly overlapping them and with some of them diagonal, until every bit of the bangle is covered. Leave to dry completely.

**7** Cut four strips from the same sheet of wrapping paper the width of the inside of the bangle and about $2\frac{3}{4}$in (7cm) in length.

**8** Using the same technique as before, stick the strips of paper on the inside of the bangle to cover it completely. Smooth the strips down but don't worry if there a few wrinkles; it is less important on the inside. Leave to dry.

**9** Finish with a coat of clear varnish to seal the paper.

WHEN CHOOSING THE WRAPPING PAPER IMAGES FOR YOUR BANGLE, STICK TO COMPLEMENTARY COLORS, STYLES, OR THEMES TO PRODUCE A SEAMLESS DESIGN.

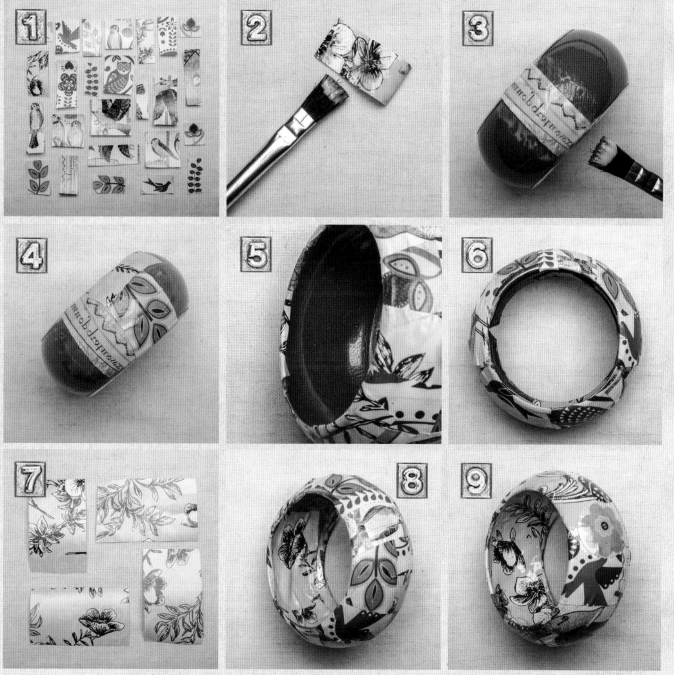

# charm

This quirky bracelet
uses pretty charms
and chunky beads
of different sizes,
shapes, and materials
to create an eclectic,
vintage feel.

# Everything you will need...

You will need plenty of bird charms and beads to build this beautifully layered bracelet.

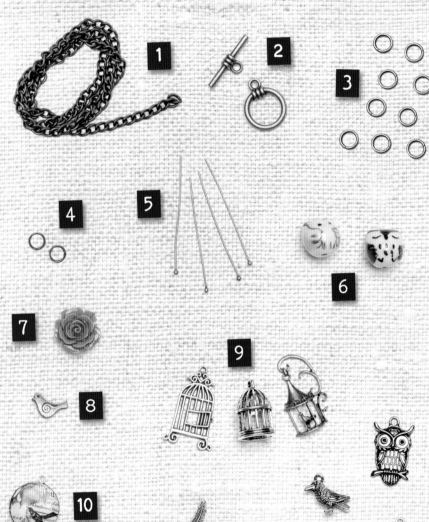

1 7in (18cm) antique gold-colored heavy curb chain (7mm x 5mm link size)

2 Antique gold-colored T-bar and end ring

3 9 x 5mm antique gold-colored jumprings

4 2 x 8mm antique gold-colored jumprings

5 4 x antique gold-colored headpins

6 2 x ceramic owl beads

7 Plastic rose bead

8 Tiny metal bird bead

9 3 x birdcage charms

10 Enameled locket charm

11 Tiny feather charm

12 4 x bird charms: owl, raven, patterned bird, swallow

Cutters

Flat-nose pliers

Round-nose pliers

charm

# Assembling the bracelet

1 Using the cutters, cut a piece of chain to 6in (15cm) in length. If your wrist is larger than average, try 6$\frac{1}{2}$in (16cm), or smaller than average, try 5$\frac{1}{2}$in (14cm).

2 Open the two 8mm jumprings (see page 18). Using one of the jumprings, attach the end ring to one end of the chain and repeat at the other end with the other jumpring and the T-bar.

3 Take an owl bead, thread it onto a headpin, and attach to the fourth link from the end ring using the wrapped loop technique (see page 19).

4 Thread the second owl bead, the tiny bird bead, and the rose bead onto the remaining headpins. Attach the owl bead to the fifth link from the T-bar, the bird bead to the eighth link from the end ring, and the rose to the sixteenth link from the end ring.

5 Take the three birdcage charms and, using 5mm jumprings, attach one to the first link from the end ring, one to the twelfth link from the end ring, and one to the nineteenth link from the end ring. Try to make sure the charms all face the same way.

6 Next, counting from the T-bar and continuing with 5mm jumprings, attach the flat owl to the first link, the raven to the third link, the enamelled locket to the ninth link, and the swallow to the eleventh link.

7 Finally, count from the end ring this time and attach the colorful bird to the sixth link and the tiny feather to the tenth link.

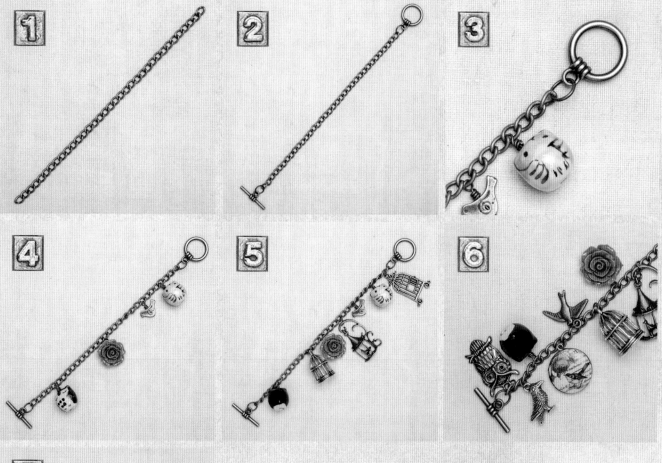

FOR A DIFFERENT STYLE, CHANGE THE COLORS OF THE CHAIN AND CHARMS. TRY SILVER AND PEARL BEADS FOR A TRADITIONAL LOOK OR BRIGHTLY COLORED PLASTICS FOR A FUNKY MODERN BRACELET.

charm

# pearly

A beautiful bird's nest, especially when
filled with tiny eggs, is a symbol of
hope, love, nurture, and protection.

# Everything you will need...

The key to this design is the delicate nature of the nest, so you'll need to work carefully to achieve the right look.

1. 60in (1.52m) length of 0.4mm (SWG 27, AWG 26) brass wire
2. 12in (30cm) length of 0.8mm (SWG 21, AWG 20) brass wire
3. 3 x pearl beads
4. Snipe-nose or flat-nose pliers
5. End cutters

pearly

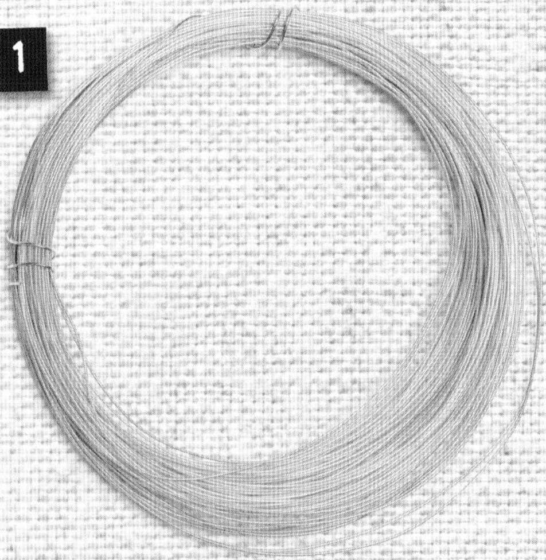

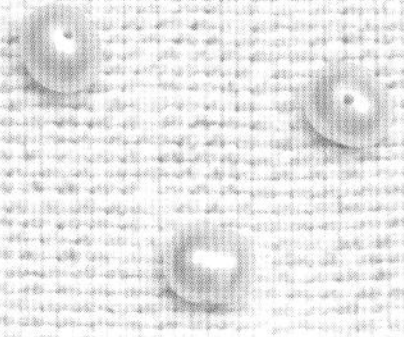

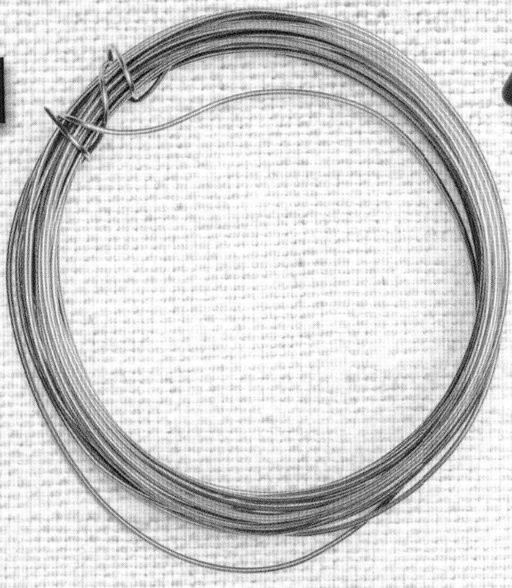

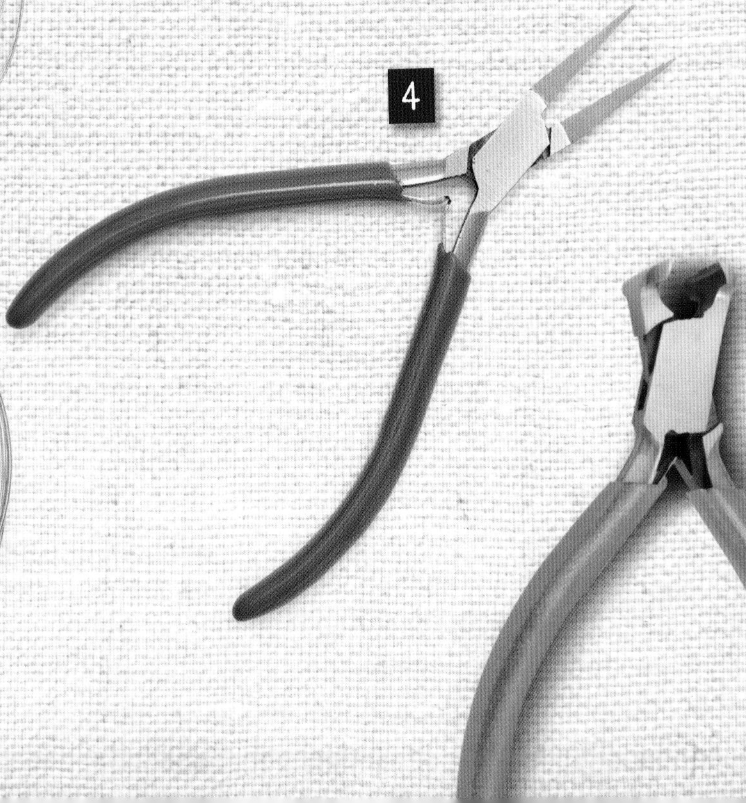

# Assembling the ring

**1** Thread the three pearl beads onto one end of the 0.4mm wire and about 8in (20cm) along the length. Push the pearls together into a triangle and twist the two ends tightly together three times. This will leave you with one really long end and one shorter end of wire.

**2** Using your fingers, make kinks along the whole length of the long end. Next, wrap this long end of wire closely around the edge of the pearls in a circle. You will have to hold onto the wire as you form the circles as they will want to spring out of shape! Wrap it around the pearls at least five times.

> USE PLIERS TO WRAP THE LOOPS AROUND THE WIRE SO YOU CAN PULL THE LOOPS TIGHT AND KEEP THEM CLOSE TOGETHER.

**3** Thread the long end under the nest and up through the middle but to the left of the pearls. Wrap the wire around in this place twice more. Make a half circle with the wire around to the opposite side of the nest and repeat the threading.

**4** Turn the nest over and, again with the long end of wire, wrap it around in circles of different sizes until the bottom is covered and you are left with a piece approximately 7in (18cm) long.

**5** Thread this end over the top of the nest and down through the center, making sure to go through the circle of wire attached to the pearls, and wrap again like this twice more. Repeat on the opposite side of the nest. Do these wraps away from those in step 3 to secure the nest in four different places.

**6** Find the center of the 0.8mm wire, rest it on your chosen finger, and wind each end of the wire once around your finger to make three loops.

**7** Take the wire off your finger. Take one end of wire and, using your pliers, wrap it around all three loops tightly, twice. Using the end cutters, snip off the excess wire and tuck the end neatly against the wraps. Repeat with the other side of the wire.

**8** Place the nest on top of the ring in the middle of the wraps and hold in place. Using the excess wire on the nest, thread it in between two of the loops in the ring and up through the middle of the nest and back around but in between the other two loops the second time. Keep going until the wire is all used and tuck the end into the nest.

**9** Repeat on the opposite side of the ring.

YOU COULD USE TURQUOISE BEADS AND SILVER WIRE TO CREATE A VERSION OF A ROBIN'S NEST AND EGGS.

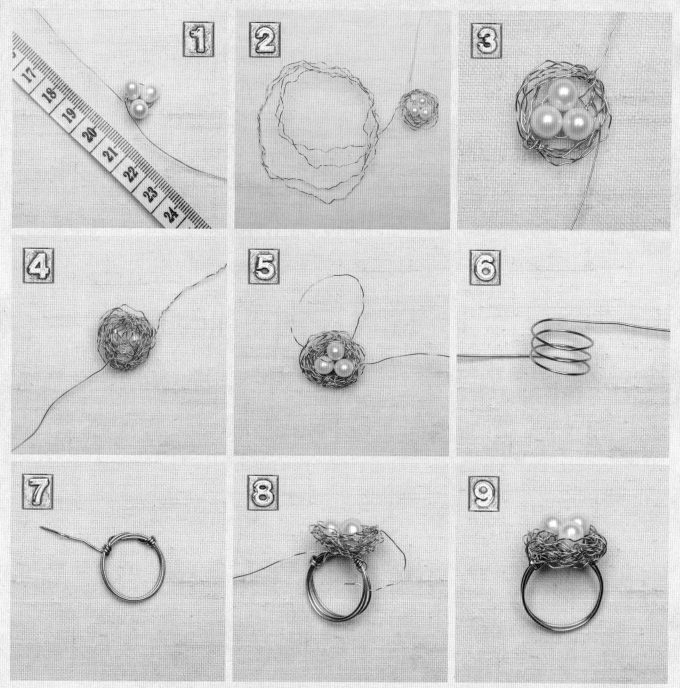

pearly
------

# peacock

A scanned image of a peacock
feather glued into a bezel and
topped with a glass dome creates
a simple but stylish ring.

# Everything you will need...

Use the photo here in the bezel or your own printed picture, collage, Inkjet-printed picture, or piece of fabric.

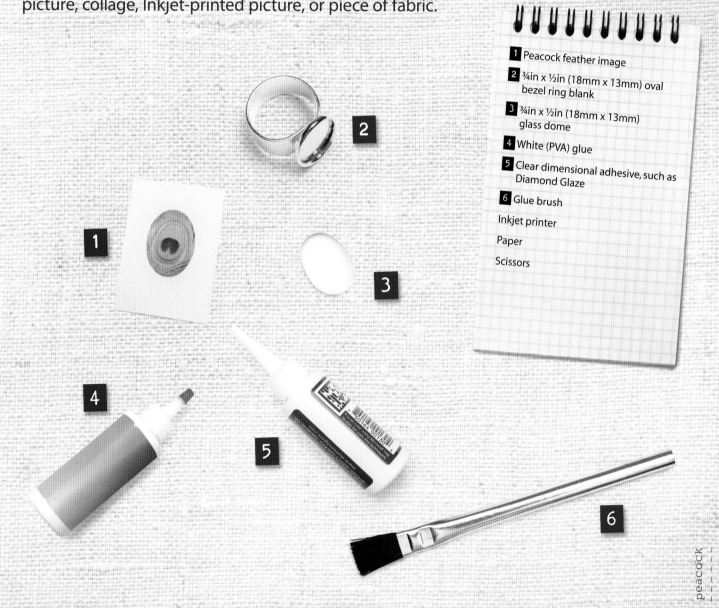

1. Peacock feather image
2. ¾in x ½in (18mm x 13mm) oval bezel ring blank
3. ¾in x ½in (18mm x 13mm) glass dome
4. White (PVA) glue
5. Clear dimensional adhesive, such as Diamond Glaze
6. Glue brush

Inkjet printer

Paper

Scissors

# Assembling the ring

**1** Scan the peacock feather image and print it out, then water down a small amount of white glue and paint over the whole image. Allow to dry, then add another two coats. This is to stop the ink from running.

**2** Cut the image out so it fits into the ring bezel.

**3** Coat the back of the image with clear dimensional adhesive and stick inside the ring bezel. Leave to dry for about 10 minutes.

**4** Cover the front of the image with more clear dimensional adhesive.

**5** Press the glass dome down firmly on top of the image. Make sure there are no bubbles and then leave to dry thoroughly before wearing.

DO NOT SHAKE THE CLEAR DIMENSIONAL ADHESIVE BEFORE USING AS THIS WILL CREATE BUBBLES UNDER THE GLASS.

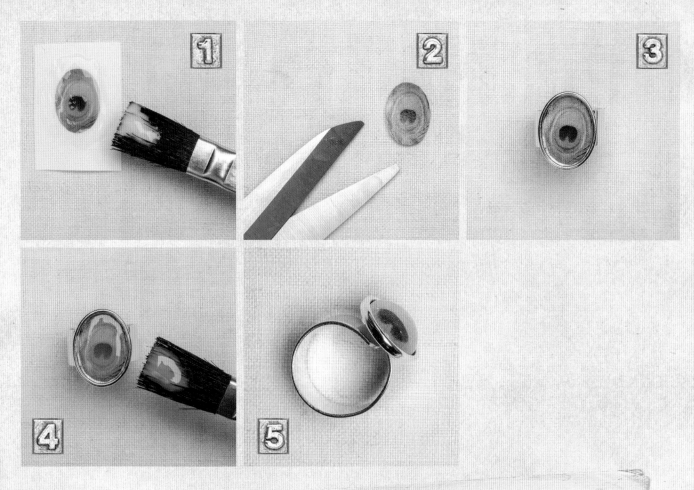

IF YOU ARE USING A DIFFERENT IMAGE FROM THE ONE PROVIDED AND NEED TO GET THE CORRECT SIZE, TAKE YOUR GLASS DOME, PLACE IT ON THE PART OF THE IMAGE YOU LIKE, DRAW AROUND IT, AND THEN CUT IT OUT SLIGHTLY INSIDE THE LINES.

# brooches and cufflinks

# night owl

Metallic-effect, dark-colored clay
gives these stylish cufflinks a
masculine edge. There are numerous
other colors available to try.

# Everything you will need...

Polymer clay is is hard-wearing and lightweight, which makes it ideal for jewelry. Widely available in craft and toy stores, it is easy to work with and can be baked in a domestic oven.

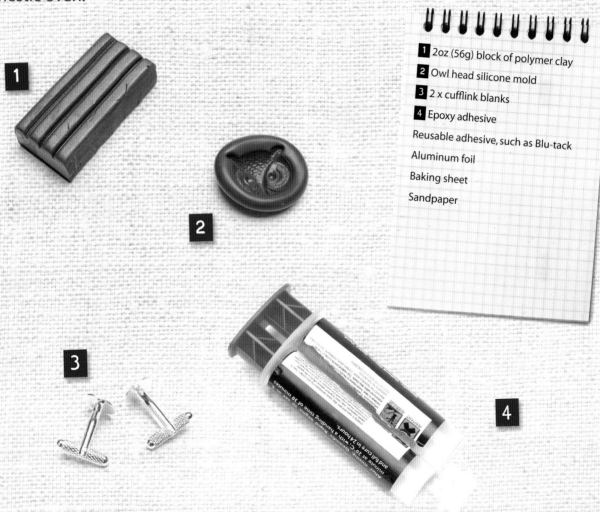

1. 2oz (56g) block of polymer clay
2. Owl head silicone mold
3. 2 x cufflink blanks
4. Epoxy adhesive

Reusable adhesive, such as Blu-tack

Aluminum foil

Baking sheet

Sandpaper

# Assembling the cufflinks

1 Take half a strip of polymer clay and knead it on a work surface until it is really warm and soft.

2 Roll into a ball and flatten out into a disk shape. Measure it up to the mold and try to make the clay no bigger than the owl head. You may need to remove some of the clay at this point.

3 Keeping the mold flat, push and shape the clay into it, covering all of the owl head, including the ears. Try not to go too far outside of the owl detail with the clay and also keep the back as flat as possible.

4 Put the mold and clay into the freezer for 2 minutes to harden up. This will make it easier to remove from the mold without losing any detail. Carefully remove the clay from the mold and repeat steps 1–4 to make the second cufflink.

5 Place both clay heads onto a foil-lined baking sheet and put into a cold oven. Turn the oven on to 200°F (100°C) and bake the clay for about 15 minutes, then turn it up to 230°F (110°C) for another 15 minutes. Turn off the oven and let the pieces cool in there.

6 Sandpaper the flat disk on the cufflink blanks slightly to create a rough surface for the glue to adhere to.

7 Mix some two-part epoxy adhesive (see page 24) and spread it evenly onto the flat disks. Put a small blob of adhesive in the center of the back of the owl head.

8 Place the cufflink blanks onto the back of the owl heads and press and hold for a minute. Use a piece of reusable adhesive or polymer clay to support the cufflinks and keep them level. Leave for at least 14 hours before wearing, to be certain the epoxy adhesive is set.

SILICONE IS OVENPROOF, SO YOU DON'T NEED TO REMOVE YOUR CLAY FROM THE MOLD BEFORE BAKING IT.

BEFORE YOU PUT POLYMER CLAY IN THE OVEN, COVER IT WITH A FOIL 'TENT'. TAKE A PIECE OF FOIL THAT WILL COVER THE CLAY, FOLD IT IN HALF, THEN OPEN OUT SLIGHTLY TO FORM AN UPSIDE-DOWN 'V' SHAPE. PLACE OVER THE CLAY SO IT DOES NOT TOUCH IT.

# victoriana

This stylish brooch inspired
by the Victorian era makes
the perfect finishing touch
to any outfit.

# Everything you will need...

Silhouettes from magazines, photos, drawings, or even cutouts from fabric are all suitable for making this stylish Victorian-style brooch.

1 Bronze flat-backed bezel

2 Printed image

3 Brooch pin

4 Scissors

5 White (PVA) glue or clear dimensional adhesive, such as Diamond Glaze

6 Glue brush

Two-part epoxy resin, such as Envirotex Lite

Epoxy adhesive

1

2

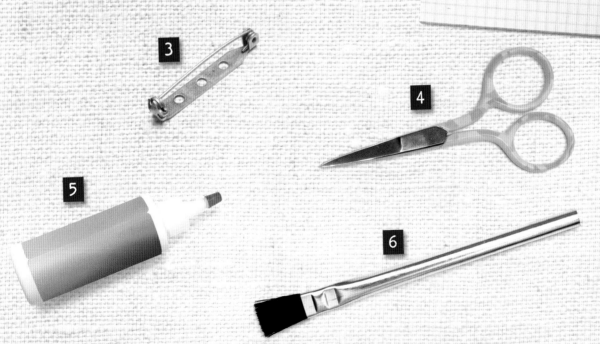

3

4

5

6

# Assembling the brooch

**1** Find your own image, or scan and print the image on page 85. Cut it out, and check that it fits into the bezel. If you are using a different image, place the bezel on the image and draw around the inside rim.

**2** Paint the front and sides of your image with glue. Leave it to dry and then turn it over and repeat on the back and sides. Do this twice to be sure it is completely sealed.

**3** When the image is dry, put a tiny blob of white (PVA) glue or clear dimensional adhesive such as Diamond Glaze onto the back of it and press into the bezel so it is completely flat.

**4** Mix the two-part epoxy resin (see page 22) and pour into the bezel on top of the image. Leave to dry for at least 24 hours.

**5** Mix some epoxy adhesive (see page 24). Cover the brooch pin with glue, and also a vertical line down the middle of the bezel back where you will stick the pin. Make sure the pin runs parallel with your bird image so it is the right way up when attached to clothing.

**6** Stick the brooch pin onto the back of the bezel and leave to dry flat for at least 8 hours.

WHEN USING A FABRIC OR PAPER IMAGE,
ALWAYS SEAL IT WITH WHITE (PVA) GLUE
BEFORE POURING THE RESIN INTO THE BEZEL
SO THAT THE RESIN DOES NOT DAMAGE IT.

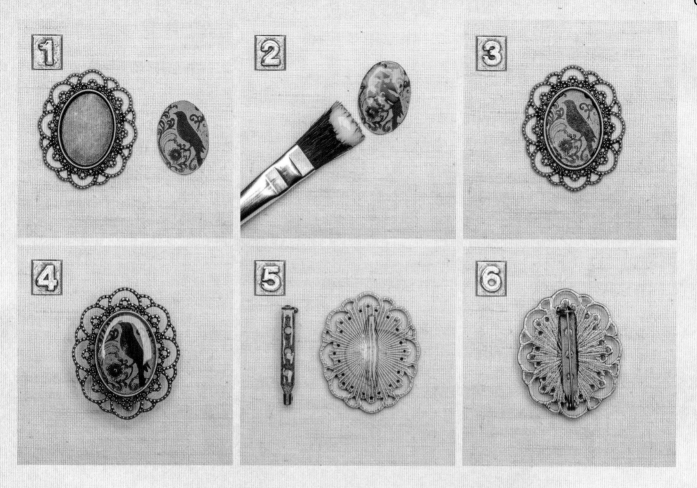

THE KEY TO GOOD RESULTS IS TO STORE AND WORK WITH
THE RESIN IN A WARM ROOM. THE RESIN CAN BECOME CLOUDY
IF IT GETS TOO COLD. AND THE WARMER THE ROOM THE
QUICKER IT CURES (HARDENS).

victoriana
- - - - -

# elegance

These antique silver swallows bring
an eye-catching finishing touch to
classic buttoned-up shirt collars.

# Everything you will need...

Collar pins can be worn by both men and women. Simply choose charms and chains to suit the person who will be wearing them.

**1** Pin and clutch-back blanks

**2** 2 x swallow charms

**3** 6¾in (17cm) silver curb chain (5mm x 3.5mm link size)

**4** 2 x silver 5mm jumprings

Epoxy adhesive

Flat- or snipe-nose pliers

Cutters

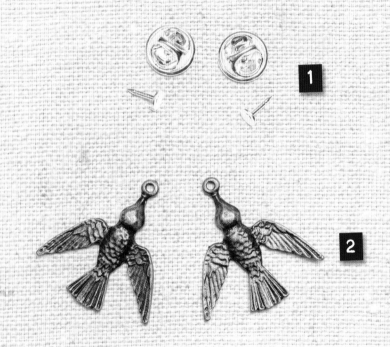

THESE PIN AND
CLUTCH-BACK BLANKS
CAN ALSO BE USED TO
CREATE A SIMPLE PIN
BROOCH OR BADGE.

# Assembling the collar pins

**1** Mix some epoxy adhesive and apply a generous amount to the disks on the two pins.

**2** Turn the two swallow charms onto their backs and put a blob of the adhesive in the center of each swallow charm. Using pliers, pick up the pins and stick in the center of the charm on top of the adhesive. Leave to dry for 8 hours before handling.

**3** Using the cutters, cut one piece of chain to 2³⁄₄in (7cm) and another piece to 4in (10cm).

**4** Open the 5mm jumprings (see page 18) and thread through the loops on the swallow charms.

**5** Thread the ends of the 4-in (10-cm) chain onto the jumprings first and then thread the ends of the 2³⁄₄in (7-cm) chain onto them.

**6** Close the jumprings and put the backs onto the pins. The collar pins are now ready to be attached to your collars.

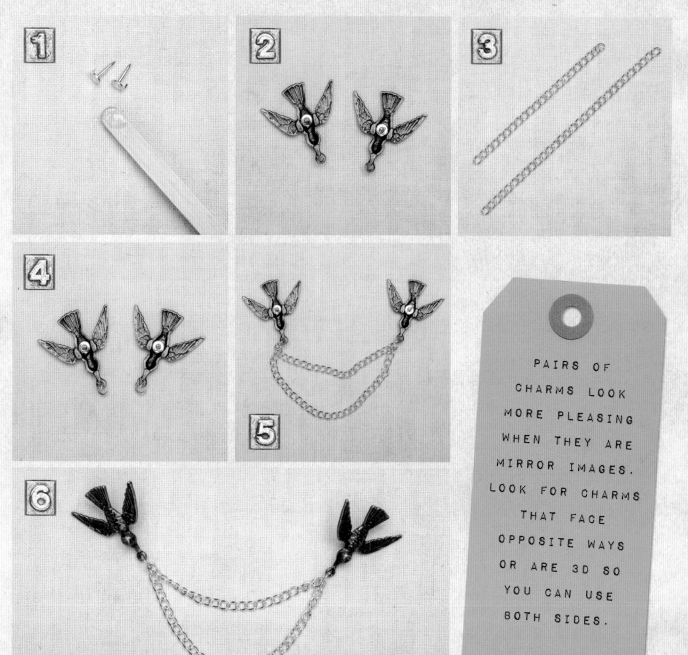

PAIRS OF
CHARMS LOOK
MORE PLEASING
WHEN THEY ARE
MIRROR IMAGES.
LOOK FOR CHARMS
THAT FACE
OPPOSITE WAYS
OR ARE 3D SO
YOU CAN USE
BOTH SIDES.

# flamingo

Think pink with this pretty felt brooch. Different shades of pink buttons in lots of sizes, shapes, and finishes add a lovely quirky edge to this classic figure.

# Everything you will need...

Felt is the ideal fabric for this easy project as the edges won't fray and it is available in lots of bright colors.

**1** Flamingo template

**2** 6in x 5in (15cm x 12cm) light pink felt

**3** 2½in x 2½in (6cm x 6cm) dark pink felt

**4** 18 x assorted buttons

**5** Reel of white cotton

**6** Brooch pin

Paper scissors

Fabric scissors

Needle

White (PVA) glue

Glue brush

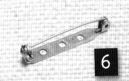

flamingo

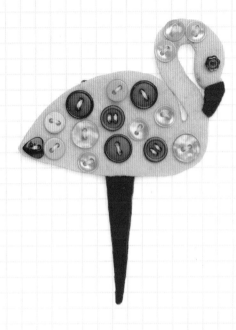

# Assembling the brooch

**1** Scan and print or photocopy the patterns on page 93 and use paper scissors to cut them out. Then, using fabric scissors, follow the patterns to cut out two flamingo bodies from the light pink felt and the two legs and beak from the dark pink felt.

**2** Place all of the buttons onto one of the flamingo bodies in a design you are happy with. Then, using the needle and thread, sew each button into place. Don't worry about the back of the felt looking untidy, as it will be covered up.

**3** Take the second felt body and turn it over to face the opposite direction to the body with the buttons on. Sew the brooch pin onto this side of the body, in the middle near to the top.

**4** Cover one side of each leg with white (PVA) glue and stick them together, glue side inward.

**5** Cover the back of the button-covered body with glue and place the top of the legs in the middle, $1/4$in (5mm) up from the bottom of it.

**6** Cover the back of the second body with glue and stick on top of the first body, glue-covered sides together, trapping the legs between them.

**7** Cover the back of the dark pink felt beak with glue and stick onto the flamingo, in the beak space. Allow the glue to dry overnight before wearing the brooch.

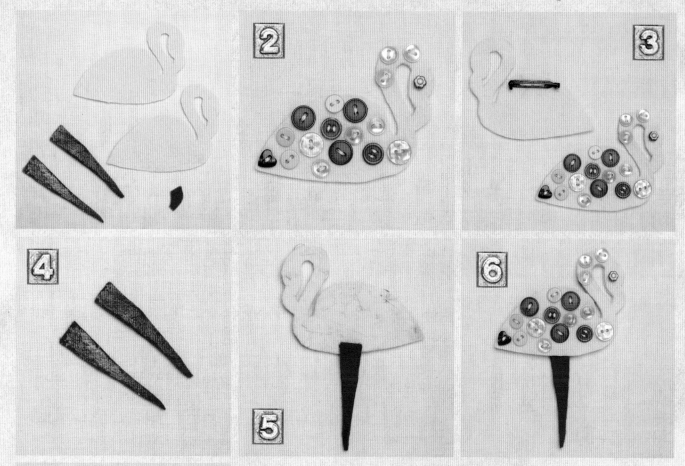

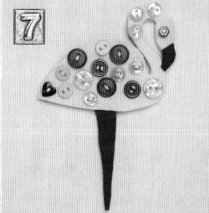

YOU CAN USE WHITE (PVA) GLUE TO STICK
BUTTONS TO THE FELT. IF YOU DO, LEAVE THE
GLUE TO DRY COMPLETELY BEFORE CONTINUING
THE REST OF THE PROJECT.

flamingo

accessories

# streamlined

This stunning hair accessory captures the style and elegance displayed by many of our feathered friends and is very simple to make.

# Everything you will need...

This project uses feathers ready bound with tiny decorative feathers at the base. The ends are neatly finished in black tape.

**1** 8in x 8in (20cm x 20cm) black felt

**2** 3 x burgundy craft feathers

**3** 3 x ready-bound feathers

**4** 2 x tiny peacock feathers

**5** Black fabric-covered headband

Fabric scissors

Glue gun

streamlined

# Assembling the headband

**1** Cut two identical teardrop shapes out of the black felt, approximately 5in (13cm) long by 3in (7.5cm) at the widest point.

**2** Position your three burgundy feathers at the top of the felt, in a fan shape, with the middle feather slightly higher than the other two. Make sure you can't see any of the felt at the top or sides of the feathers.

**3** Put a line of hot glue onto the felt underneath each feather. Press and hold each feather for a few minutes to ensure it is secure.

**4** Cover the remaining felt in a good amount of hot glue and place your three ready bound feathers, again in a fan shape, onto the glue and press and hold. Also put a tiny blob underneath the top of each feather and press down to secure to the feathers underneath.

**5** Cut two small peacock feathers to about 3in (7.5cm). Put a small blob of hot glue on the end of each one and slide down behind the tiny feathers at the base of the thinner feathers. Also put a blob of hot glue on the feather underneath the top of each peacock feather and press and hold.

**6** Squeeze a thick line of hot glue all the way along the underside of your feather decoration.

**7** Place the decoration onto the headband approximately 2–2½in (5–6cm) from the end, so the glue runs along it. Press down hard and hold both ends down until the glue sets. Don't worry if the glue spills out onto the felt.

**8** Cover the second piece of felt with hot glue but not quite to the edges as you don't want it to ooze out of the sides.

**9** Match up to the felt on the back of your decoration, place down and gently press, and hold until the glue has dried.

IF THE BASE OF YOUR FEATHER DECORATION LOOKS UNTIDY WITH LOTS OF FEATHER ENDS SHOWING, FIND A PRETTY BUTTON LARGE ENOUGH TO COVER IT AND SIMPLY HOT GLUE IT ON TOP.

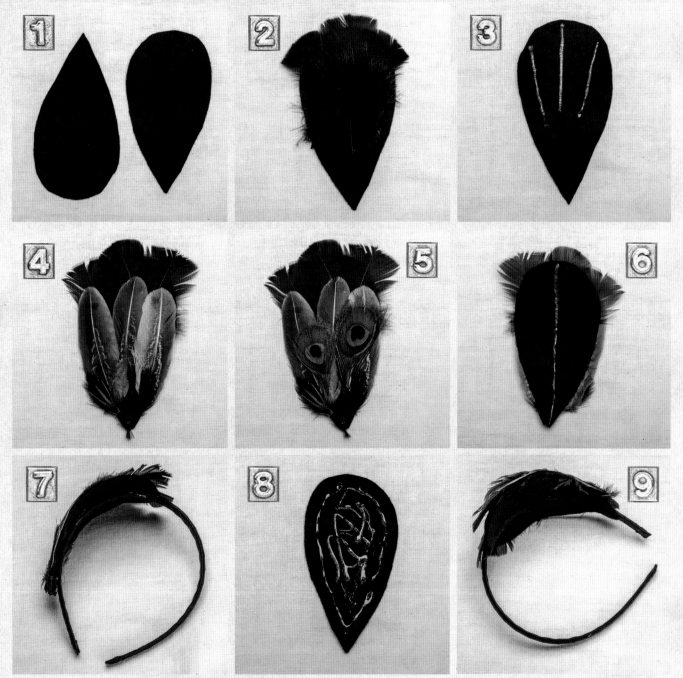

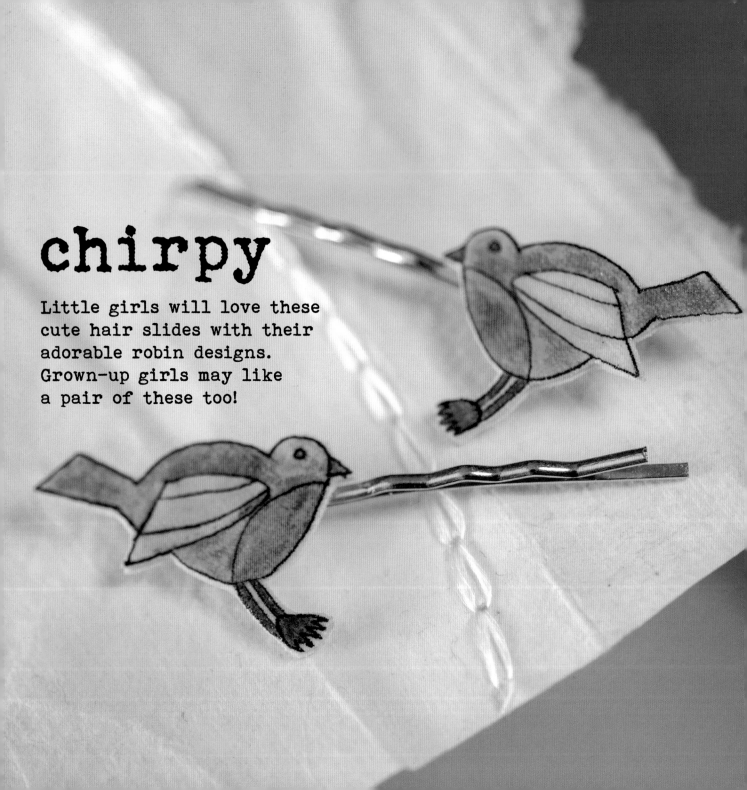

# chirpy

Little girls will love these
cute hair slides with their
adorable robin designs.
Grown-up girls may like
a pair of these too!

# Everything you will need...

I have used coloring pencils but you can also use permanent markers, acrylic paints, heat-set paint/inks with rubber stamps, and felt tips to draw on and color the shrink plastic.

1 Robins template
2 White shrink plastic
3 2 x blank hair slides
4 Fine-grade sandpaper
5 Fine-line marker pen
6 Colored pencils

Scissors

Parchment paper

Baking sheet

Clear dimensional adhesive, such as Diamond Glaze

Glue brush

Epoxy adhesive

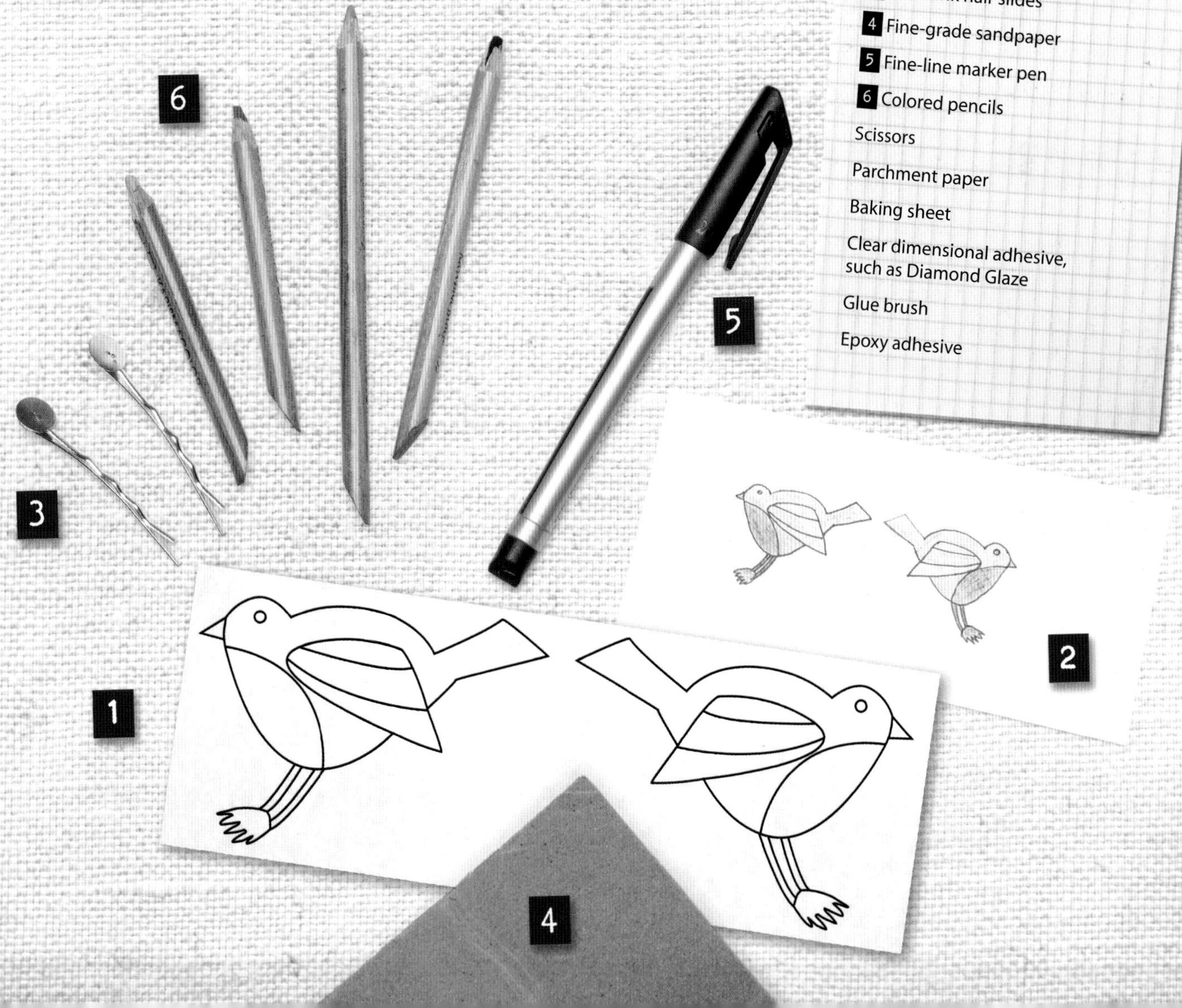

# Assembling the hair slides

**1** Sand the shrink plastic with fine-grade sandpaper in a crisscross pattern. This is so the coloring pencils will work on the plastic.

**2** Place the shrink plastic over the bird pattern. Using a fine-line marker pen, trace the images.

**3** When the pen has dried completely, color the images in with your choice of coloring pencils.

**4** Cut around each bird about $^1/_{32}$in (1mm) from the edge of its lines.

**5** Line a baking sheet with parchment paper, place the birds on the paper and cover with another piece of parchment paper. Bake in the oven for 2–3 minutes (see page 20).

**6** When shrunk, remove the earrings from the oven and leave to cool. To seal your printed design, after baking, coat the earrings with a thin coat of clear dimensional adhesive and leave them to dry.

**7** Mix some epoxy adhesive (see page 24) and put a blob on the disk of the blank hair slide and a blob on the center back of the bird.

**8** Place the disk of the hair slide on top of the bird, press and hold for a moment, and then leave to dry for about 8 hours. Repeat steps 7 and 8 for the second hair slide.

THE SHRINK FILM WILL NOT ALWAYS SHRINK PERFECTLY IN PROPORTION AND NO TWO PIECES WILL EVER BE IDENTICAL. REMEMBER TO ALLOW FOR SOME DISTORTION AND CONSIDER IT A BONUS THAT EACH PIECE WILL BE UNIQUE.

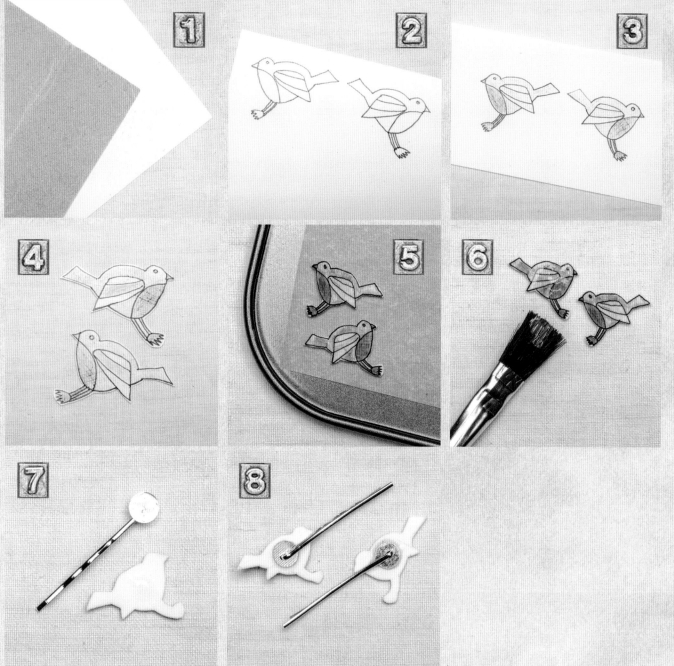

# sparkly

For eye-catching glamour, add a touch of sparkle to your outfit with this beautiful beaded comb. It's the ideal hair accessory for any special occasion.

# Everything you will need...

Take your time and aim to keep this design neat.
Remember, the wire is functional and should be
tucked away behind the decoration.

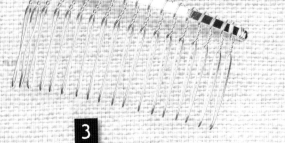

1. Diamanté bird brooch
2. 0.4mm (SWG 27, AWG 26) silver-plated craft wire
3. Comb
4. 3 x 7mm pearl beads
5. 4 x 6mm pearl beads
6. 4 x 6mm clear crystal-shape beads
7. 4 x 4mm pewter-colored beads

Superglue

Tape measure

Cutters

Flat- or snipe-nose pliers

sparkly

# Assembling the comb

**1** Fasten the brooch pin and ensure the catch is in the closed position. Then squeeze a generous amount of superglue all over the catch and the end of the pin so it will no longer open. Leave to dry completely.

**2** Cut 23²/₃in (60cm) of wire. Measure 1¹/₂in (4cm) in from one end and, starting from that point, wrap the end of the wire tightly around the top brooch fastening. Then guide the long piece of wire to the bottom fastening and wrap it around tightly at least three times.

AFTER WRAPPING, ALWAYS TUCK IN THE END OF EACH PIECE OF WIRE TO PREVENT SHARP BITS STABBING THE WEARER.

**3** Now wrap the leftover wire around the outside of both fastenings four times and finally once more around the bottom fastening to secure. Fold the remaining attached wire in half and twist together until the stem is 2¹/₂in (6cm) long. Cut off excess wire.

**4** Hold the bird above the top of the comb so the twisted wire stem comes down over the top of it. Leave about ¹/₂in (1cm) of the twisted wire above the top of the comb and wrap the rest of it around it.

**5** Cut another 5¹/₂in (14cm) length of wire, cut it in half, and twist the two pieces together. Then wrap the end of it tightly three times around the bottom half of the bird's tail. Again, leave a ½-in (1-cm) length of wire above the top of the comb, and then wrap the rest of the wire from the tail around the comb.

**6** Cut a 3¹/₄-in (8-cm) piece of wire and thread one small pearl, one clear, and one pewter bead halfway along it. Bend the wire around so the ends cross over each other and the beads are now in a circle. Twist the wire together at the bottom.

**7** Take this three-bead wire and measure ¹/₂in (1cm) in from the end of the comb. Leave a piece of wire so the beads stand up away from the comb a bit and then wrap the remaining wire around the top of the comb.

**8** Cut a piece of wire 23²/₃in (60cm) long and wrap the end of it around the end of the comb about four times. Thread a large pearl bead all the way along the wire until it reaches the comb, hold it in place, and then wrap the long wire twice around the top of the comb next to the bead.

**9** Add the next bead and repeat. Keep adding and wrapping until the whole top of the comb is covered.

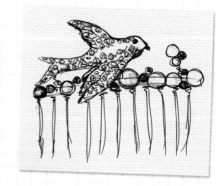

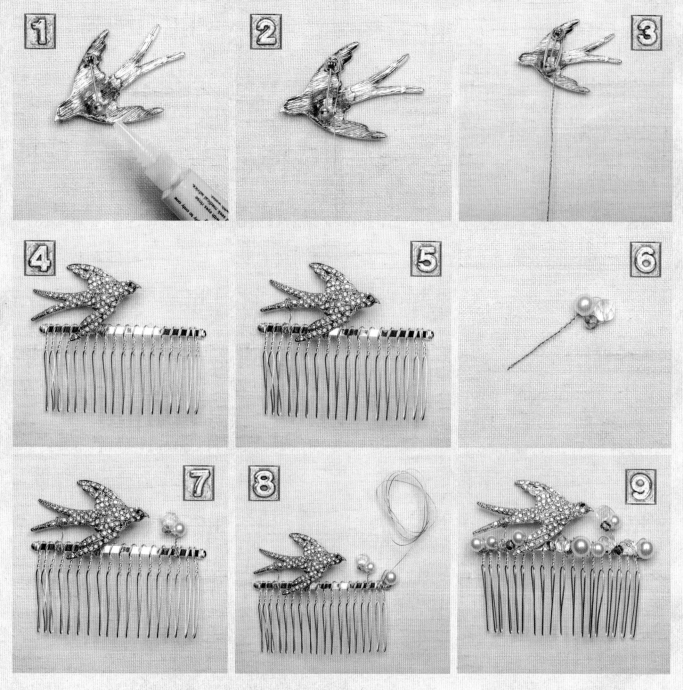

# vintage

Attach this adorable little fellow to your keys to keep them safe! Hand stitching gives this cute owl keyring an individual rustic charm all of his own.

# Everything you will need...

Try to use scraps or recycled fabrics for a truly vintage feel. Rather than buying pillow stuffing, cut up an old cushion and reuse the insides.

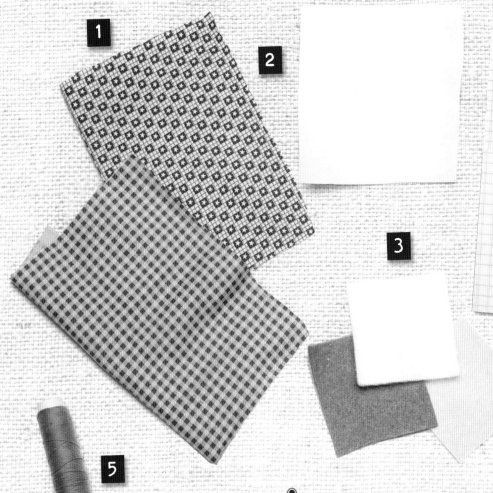

**1** 10in x 10in (25cm x 25cm) of star fabric and checked fabric

**2** 10in x 10in (25cm x 25cm) of double-sided fabric adhesive, such as Wonder Under

**3** 1½in x 1½in (4cm x 4cm) of white, green, and pink felt

**4** 2 x seed beads

**5** Reel of green thread

**6** 2¾in (7cm) ribbon

**7** Split ring for keyring

1¾oz (50g) pillow stuffing

Reel of invisible thread

Paper

Fabric scissors

Needle

# Assembling the keyring

**1** Using the templates (see below), cut out two bodies of the owl in the star fabric, one belly in the checked fabric and fabric adhesive, the two large eyes in white felt and fabric adhesive, the two small eyes in green felt and fabric adhesive, and the beak in pink felt and fabric adhesive.

**2** Put one body on top of the other with both patterned sides facing inwards towards each other. Start ³⁄₄in (2cm) down from the top of the ear and draw a line about ³⁄₁₆in (4mm) from the edge around the body and to the same point on the other side. Take the needle and thread and backstitch all the way along the line, finishing with a knot. Turn the body inside out.

**3** Take the belly and the matching fabric adhesive and iron onto the body just above the bottom and in the center. Again, using the fabric adhesive, iron on the two large felt eyes just above each side of the top of the belly. Then, with fabric adhesive, iron the small eyes on top of the larger eyes, and finally iron on the beak and fabric adhesive directly below the eyes.

**4** Next, using green thread and starting from behind the eyes, stitch one seed bead into the center of each of the smaller green eyes.

**5** Fill your owl to the top with the pillow stuffing until it is nice and plump.

**6** Thread the keyring onto the ribbon and find the middle. Then, using a tiny piece of fabric adhesive, iron the two ends together.

**7** Insert the ribbon into the top of the owl between the ears and hold in place. Using invisible thread, whipstitch around the top of the owl's first ear, then change to backstitch when you reach the ribbon and sew across it. Change back to whipstitch for the second ear. Finish with a knot and trim the thread.

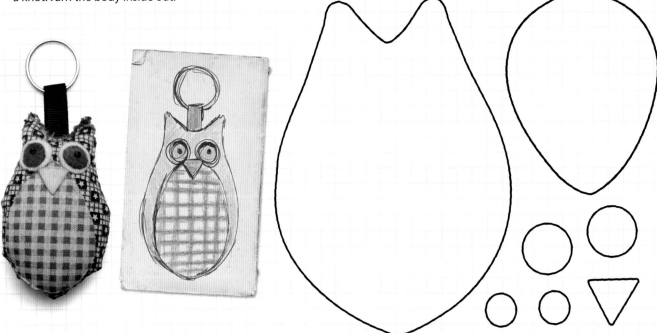

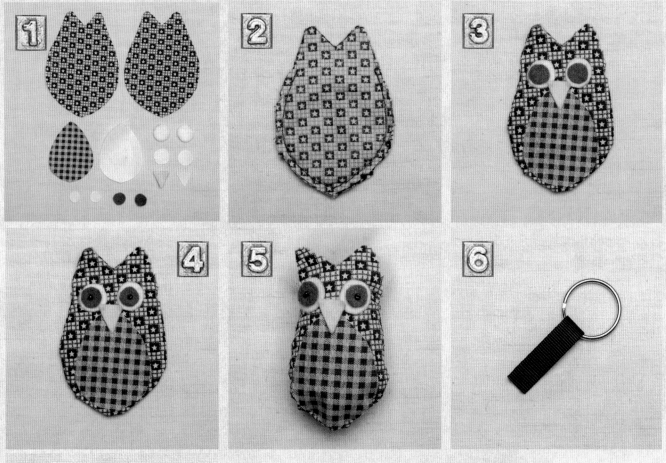

MAKE YOUR STITCHES QUITE SHORT AND CLOSE TOGETHER TO CREATE STRONG SEAMS TO KEEP THE STUFFING SAFELY INSIDE THE OWL.

vintage

# retro

This simple yet effective technique allows you to create beautifully finished and highly original fabric cuff designs.

# Everything you will need...

For a more intricate design, you can add more layers of fabric and cut out more shapes, but remember to keep your shapes simple so you can cut them out easily.

1. Peacock cuff template
2. 10in x 39½in (25cm x 100cm) each of denim, pink cotton, and peacock patterned fabric
3. 10in x 39½in (25cm x 100cm) double-sided fabric adhesive, such as Wonder Under
4. 2 x tiny snap fasteners

Tape measure

Fabric scissors

Inkjet printer

Paper scissors

Pencil or felt-tip pen

Iron

Needle and dark blue thread

retro

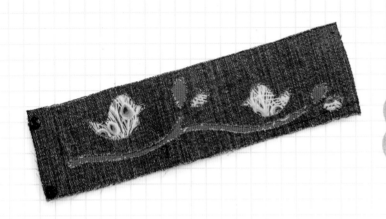

I USED DENIM IN THIS DESIGN TO ADD STIFFNESS TO THE CUFF SO IT KEEPS ITS SHAPE AND HAS A HARDWEARING OUTER LAYER. OTHER THICK MATERIALS SUCH AS LEATHER, FELT, OR CORDUROY ARE EQUALLY EFFECTIVE.

# Assembling the cuff

**1** Measure your wrist with the tape measure and then add an extra $\frac{1}{2}$in (1.5cm). Using fabric scissors, cut a strip of fabric to this length, with a width of 2in (5cm). Repeat on the other two fabrics and two pieces of double-sided fabric adhesive.

**2** Scan and print the birds and leaves and cut them out using paper scissors. Put the denim fabric face down and place the shapes in a mirror image of how you want them to look when the fabric is turned over. Draw around the shapes and draw branches to complete the design.

**3** Using fabric scissors, snip a hole in the middle of each shape and cut it out from there.

**4** Turn the denim fabric over and place directly on top of the pink fabric. Using the denim as a stencil, draw through the bird shapes and two of the leaf shapes that you don't want to be pink. Cut out the bird and leaf shapes slightly larger than the outline so no pink is seen through the denim.

**5** Place the cut-out denim fabric on top of one piece of the fabric adhesive, with the paper side facing up, and draw through all of the shapes onto the fabric adhesive beneath. Cut out the shapes from the fabric adhesive, iron it onto the back of the denim, and peel off the paper backing (see page 25). Repeat with the pink fabric.

**6** Take the peacock fabric and place the pink fabric (adhesive side first) on top of it and then the denim fabric (adhesive side first) on top of the pink fabric. Iron over this to stick them all together. Trim all edges to remove any threads and uneven fabric.

**7** Open a snap fastener and, using a needle and dark blue thread, sew one side of the fastener to the top left corner of the back of the cuff. Repeat this with a second fastener but sew to the bottom-left corner.

**8** Turn the cuff over and, on the opposite end to where you have already sewn the fasteners, sew on the matching parts to the top and bottom corner.

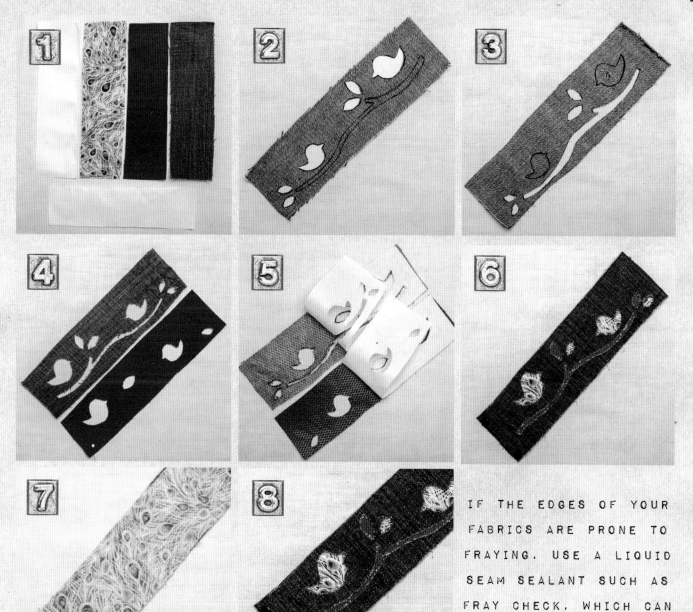

IF THE EDGES OF YOUR
FABRICS ARE PRONE TO
FRAYING, USE A LIQUID
SEAM SEALANT SUCH AS
FRAY CHECK, WHICH CAN
BE CAREFULLY APPLIED
ALONG THE EDGES.

# resources

## SOURCES OF MATERIALS

### UK

Big Bead Boutique
12 Dyke Road
Brighton
BN1 3FE
Tel: +44 (0)1273 383983
www.bigbeadboutique.co.uk

Brighton & Hove Plastics
42 Boundary Road
Hove
BN3 4EF
Tel: +44 (0)1273 421122
www.brightonandhoveplastics.co.uk

Cookson Precious Metals Ltd
59–83 Vittoria Street
Birmingham
B1 3NZ
Tel: +44 (0)845 100 1122
www.cooksongold.com

Hobbycraft
Stores Nationwide
Tel: +44 (0)1202 596100
www.hobbycraft.co.uk

Jasmin Studio Ltd
60 Madeira Road
London
SW16 2DE
www.jasminstudiocrafts.com

### USA

Charm Factory
5921 Office Blvd NE
Albuquerque NM 87109
Tel: +1 505 345 1635
www.charmfactory.com

Fire Mountain Gems
1 Fire Mountain Way
Grants Pass
OR 97526-2373
Tel: +1 541 956 7890
www.firemountaingems.com

Michaels Stores
nationwide
www.michaels.com

### AUSTRALIA

Beads Online
PO Box 160
Tweed Heads
NSW 2487
Tel: +61 (0)2 6674 4570
www.beadsonline.com.au

Over the Rainbow
PO Box 9112
Seaford
VIC 3198
Tel: +61 (0)3 9785 3800
www.polymerclay.com.au

## ONLINE SOURCES

Craft on the internet
www.craft.ontheinternet.com.au

Etsy shops: www.etsy.com
Intirado
Miniaturasdemon
Moldsrus

My Fabric House
www.myfabrichouse.co.uk

Lawrence Art Supplies
www.lawrence.co.uk

Metal Clay Ltd
www.metalclay.co.uk

Pen to Paper
www.pentopaperonline.com

## acknowledgments

I would like to say a big thank you to all of the wonderful people I have worked with or who have helped and inspired me during my years making jewelry. Also to Nathan and Daniel who have to put up with all sorts of weird and wonderful craft materials strewn all around the house!

# about the author

Sophie Robertson is a jewelry designer/maker currently living and working in Brighton in the southeast of England. Sophie has a BA Hons in Silversmithing and Jewelry Design from Loughborough University and has been designing and making her own jewelry collections for more than ten years. Her love of art and craft has also inspired her to share her knowledge and skills, and she has worked with adults and children of all ages and abilities in many different settings on a wide range of fun, craft-based, creative projects. She is also the author of *Charms*, for GMC Publications.

# index

To place an order, or request
a catalog, contact:

GMC Publications Ltd
Castle Place, 166 High Street,
Lewes, East Sussex, BN7 1XU
United Kingdom

Tel: +44 (0)1273 488005

www.gmcbooks.com